# the sex offender

# the sex offender

## by Bart Delin

BEACON PRESS    BOSTON

Beacon Press books are published under the auspices
of the Unitarian Universalist Association
Published simultaneously in Canada by
Fitzhenry & Whiteside Limited, Toronto

Printed in the United States of America

(hardcover) 9  8  7  6  5  4  3  2  1

**Library of Congress Cataloging in Publication Data**

Delin, Bart.
  The sex offender.

  1. Sex offenders—United States. 2. Sex offenders—Rehabilitation—
United States. I. Title.
HQ72.U53D44       364.1'53       78-53789
ISBN 0-8070-4154-8

To my husband, Roy, who spent many long nights reading the manuscript. His criticism was always honest, sometimes painful (to me), but ever loving.

*The mood and temper with regard to treatment of crime and criminals is, in any country, one of the most unfailing tests of its civilization.—*
Winston Churchill

# Acknowledgments

My first gratitude goes to the sex offenders and their wives, who so generously shared their lives with me. The courage it took to reveal their pain is my constant amazement. Knowing them gave me the determination to share my experiences. I have genuine affection for some and sincere respect for all. I am deeply indebted to all others who allowed me interviews. Their expertise helps give my book authenticity.

For their advice and support, I would like to express my appreciation to the Minneapolis Writers' Workshop and the Minneapolis Branch American Association of University Women Writers' Workshop. I am also grateful to my friend Bob Lyle for his initial encouragement; to Ian Macindoe, my mentor; to Pat Santleman, for her professional advice; and to Charlotte Cecil Raymond, my editor.

Other friends to whom I am indebted are: Alice Sturr for her critical listening; Kay Peterson, Shirley Karasti, and Gayle Beeman for transcribing the tapes; Jan Yetke, Mary Grabow, Mary Lou Imm, and my sister-in-law, Marge Delin, for their excellent typing. Lastly, to the members of the

AAUW Study Task Force on Sexual Behavior and the Legal System, I am grateful for giving me the opportunity to pursue my interest in the subject of sex offenders and their treatment.

# Contents

# A Personal Note

I recently asked a policeman, "What do you think should be done with sex offenders?"

"Kill them," he said. "That's the only way we'll ever get rid of them."

Such a reply may express the depth of our feelings for revenge, but it offers little practical help in dealing with a crime that causes so much anguish to its victims, to the families of its victims, and to the sex offenders themselves.

In the past, American justice has dealt harshly with the sex offender. In some eras and some locales, those even suspected of sex crimes were lynched, especially if the suspect was black and the victim white. Today we seldom execute; instead we incarcerate those who are found guilty of sex crimes. Rarely do we give the offender any treatment that might prevent a recurrence of the crime.

It is difficult for most of us to feel sympathy toward a rapist, a child molester, or a sexual offender of any kind. Names like Jack the Ripper, the California Hillside Strangler, Son of Sam, and Richard Speck evoke terrifying images. Certainly there are criminals who have shown a history of sexual behavior so violent that they probably should be kept in permanent custody. But the majority who are incarcerated eventually will be returned to society—whether or not they have been helped. If we are to protect society, we must offer help to the sex offender, not because we excuse the deed, but for the practical reason of preventing it from happening again.

In 1972 I was asked by the Minneapolis branch of the American Association of University Women to chair a two-year study to provide data and support for that group's stance on state funding for the treatment of sex offenders. This study led to the presentation of symposia cosponsored by a variety of organizations: the Minnesota League of Women Voters, the Minnesota Mental Health Association, the Saint Paul and Minneapolis YWCAs, and the Program in Human Sexuality at the University of Minnesota. The symposia, which were called "The Sex Offender: Are We All Victims?" were funded by the Minnesota Humanities Commission, and presented on eleven separate occasions during 1975 and 1976. During these events, offenders and victims came together to hear each other's stories. Legislators and law officers, psychologists and university professors expressed their opinions based upon experiences and professional background, and each group learned from the other.

Some of the information in this book is drawn from those symposia. Other information comes from interviews I've conducted with offenders, victims, and professionals throughout the United States.

During the past three and one-half years I have visited thirteen sex-offender treatment programs operating in nine cities on the East and West Coasts and in the Midwest. These programs are in penitentiaries, city jails, mental hospitals, community-based halfway houses, medical schools and private outpatient clinics. I have become acquainted with scores of sex offenders due to my travels, meeting many of them during program therapy sessions. With some I have been in constant contact; others were with me for less than an hour. At one treatment center, I stayed four days and nights. There I joined a group of seventeen sex offenders. We talked, ate, and shared their therapy.

The sex offenders who shared their experiences with me have committed the range of offenses—rape, incest, child molestation, voyeurism, and exhibitionism. Many are multiple offenders. I interviewed juvenile offenders as well as adults, and one woman, though women represent a tiny percentage of offenders. Those interviewed came from a variety of ethnic, religious, and racial backgrounds. In order to preserve the privacy of these offenders and their victims, names as well as other identifying characteristics have been changed.

In addition, I formally interviewed judges, criminal lawyers, therapists, and legislators to learn about their attitudes toward sex offenders and their views about treatment.

People often ask me how "a nice woman like you" became interested in the problems of sex offenders, since I am neither a criminologist nor a psychologist. Intellectually I have long been concerned with the disadvantaged and with the inequities of the criminal justice system. Having been reared in a white, middle-class family and neighborhood, I was shielded from contact with the "other Minneapolis." In 1972 the opportunity to become a court watcher for the Minneapolis Civil Liberties Union attracted me and, for the first time, I listened to criminal case histories. Increasingly my observations convinced me that the greatest difference between "them" and "us" is accident of birth. This experience gave me momentum to try to change public awareness.

It was as a court watcher that I first came in contact with sex offenders. My further exposure over the past few years taught me more of what they feel, what they face, and what possibilities are open to them. I have learned that the sex offender is not born antisocial; that his behavior is learned through childhood experiences. Most sex offenders can change their behavior if therapy is available and if they are willing to take advantage of it.

I believe that everyone's life is of equal value, including that of the sex offender. He is not respected by much of humanity, which considers him despicable, hopeless, and lost; he is cut off from the rest of us. We wish him to disappear through death or life imprisonment—anywhere out of sight and mind. Rehabilitation? How can we change a man who has no respect for human values and feels no love for anyone? Why should we give any thought to helping him when he is despised even by his fellow inmates? In prison, he is at the low end of the pecking order.

My experience has been self-humanizing as well as educational, for, as Dr. Richard Chilgren, former director of the Program in Human Sexuality at the University of Minnesota, once said, "I feel we must analyze what there is within *us* that makes it so difficult to view sex offenders as human beings who are deeply troubled." Their differences are more of degree than kind.

Although most of this book is concerned with sexual offenders and their treatment, it also deals with the psychological effects of rape on their victims. Attempting to understand the problem without including both parties involved is unrealistic. Sexism and violence permeate our society. The "macho" mentality is accepted, even expected: domination of women is equated with virility and manliness. It therefore is not surprising that sex offenses occur. What is surprising is our failure to recognize that we all—men and women—are responsible for creating and perpetuating this "cave-man" role for men.

The criminal justice system is discussed as well, with the contention that it is a contradiction in terms. Too often justice is served to the rich, while the poor get the sentencing. Certainly even if we execute or castrate all known sex criminals, sex crimes will not stop. For, as I hope the pages of this book will show, before there is a sex offense, there is a deeply troubled human being.

# Part One

# Who Are the Sex Offenders?

# 1

# Sexual Psychopaths and Sexual Fiends

What image comes to mind when you think of a sex offender? A large, thick-necked, pockmarked man who wears a trenchcoat, hides out in alleys, and has a look that paralyzes his victim? As Cohen and Boucher in their sex-offender studies have stated, "The man-in-the-street is convinced that the sexual criminal is insane or mentally retarded; that he is brutal, depraved, immoral and oversexed. He is a social isolate who spends his time reading 'dirty' books or haunting 'dirty' movies: a godless, brainless fellow, a 'dirty' old man, crippled or disfigured, dope addicted, and incurable. The common denominator of these misconceptions appears to be the need to make the sexual criminal an alien being; someone as different from the 'decent' upstanding citizen as possible. He doesn't think, feel, or live as they do. He shares none of the same human needs."[1]

It is not surprising that most people share this image of the sex offender, since it has been perpetuated through the years. Ninety years ago, Dr. Richard von Krafft-Ebing wrote a terrifying and powerful book entitled *Psychopathia Sexualis* (1886). It is important to review briefly his beliefs, because he was considered the most outstanding psychiatric consultant to criminal courts of his generation and his book has greatly influenced our attitudes toward sex offenders.

Krafft-Ebing's testimony in sex cases was solicited by judges throughout Europe; he therefore had a unique opportunity to learn about the most depraved sex crimes in history. He writes of rapists who dismembered, disemboweled, and/or burned the bodies of their victims. The book gives morbid details to paint the pictures more vividly. Only after having thus set the stage in the minds of his readers does Krafft-Ebing portray the nonviolent sex offenders—the voyeurs ("peeping Toms"), the exhibitionists (flashers), and the homosexuals—using *all* their case studies as examples of "psychopathia sexualis." As a result, to this day most people do not distinguish the different types of sex offenses; they tend to group all sex offenders into one category.

Krafft-Ebing was responsible for passing along other common misconceptions. Among these are the beliefs that men undoubtedly have stronger sexual appetites than women, and that women who are physically and mentally normal and appropriately educated have much less interest in sex; woman is courted for her favor, but she is always passive; her need for love is greater, but is more of the spirit than the flesh; since by nature the man is aggressive and sexual, he experiences more temptations to break laws and to become spiritually immoral.

The practice of masturbation in early years has a corrosive effect on man's nobler nature, Krafft-Ebing contends. It removes his finer motivations, leaving only carnal and other animal cravings. This general decay of morality creates an increase in sex crimes. The renowned doctor also believed that harsh sentencing of past decades tended to discourage such crimes, and that rape and incest are very often performed by men who are imbeciles and morally depraved.[2]

Menachem Amir's findings indicate that most rapists are a

danger to the community not because they are compulsive sex fiends but because they are violent and aggressive. Amir learned that rapists are usually between fifteen and twenty-four years of age,[3] are undereducated (most do not finish high school), and are economically and occupationally in the lower range of society.[4] He contends that lower-class males learn early that sexual aggressiveness can be used to compensate for their own feelings of economic and social inferiority.

Amir's book is based on an analysis of 646 rapes committed in Philadelphia between 1958 and 1960. He exploded the myth that rapists are sexually aroused by a mini-skirt or a woman's walk, like the "average American boy." They may look the same but their response is different; their motivation is assaultive. According to Amir's studies, in the majority of cases, offenders and victims lived in the same area, and their neighborhood tended also to be the site of the offense.[5]

So what are the common sex offenses? A sex offense is defined as a violation of any law which prohibits certain types of sexual behavior. Because of various legal descriptions, reliable, consistent terminology is difficult to come by. Some state legislatures, too embarrassed to accurately describe the crime, might call it "lurid, lascivious conduct," "acts against nature," "carnal knowledge," "imperiling the morals of a minor."

Sodomy in most states relates largely to homosexual acts, but it can mean anal intercourse between man and woman or bestiality (sexual relations with an animal). Statutory rape is really not rape at all in the classic sense because it refers to sexual intercourse with a consenting female who is legally under age, and this varies with the state laws. Negotiated pleas (plea bargaining) make it more difficult to pinpoint the most common sex offenses. A man charged with a grave offense such as rape is sometimes encouraged to plead guilty to a lesser crime (often indecent liberties or breaking and entering) so that the true picture of his offense is lost.

Perhaps because of the women's liberation movement, and its concern with rape and women as victims, rape has become *the* sex offense in the minds of many people. The most common sex offenses, however, are fornication, adultery, and male homosexuality (which is still considered a sex crime in most states). Historically, these offenses were bitterly punished. Today the laws are on the books but seldom enforced.

On the other extreme are the gross offenses—the rape-murders and rape-mutilations. Though these cases receive the greater share of media attention, they represent only a small fraction of a percent of sex offenses; few of these offenders are in treatment programs because they are considered to be not treatable.

Eliminating consideration of the two extremes—adultery, homosexuality and fornication on the one hand, and the rape-murder and sex-torture cases, on the other—we are left with five categories of sex offenses:

1. Rape, assault with intent to rape
2. Child molestation
3. Exhibitionism and voyeurism
4. Incest
5. Miscellaneous offenses (breaking and entering, arson, etc., in cases where there is sexual motivation)

The sex offenders who have committed these offenses are the subject of this book. They represent the majority of sex offenders, and therapy for these cases is considered appropriate by most of the treatment programs. Nevertheless, people cling to the false belief that the "sex fiend" is the typical offender, thereby perpetuating the lie that most sex offenders are beyond help.

How realistic then is this conception of the sex offender

as sex fiend? In answering the question it is important to know that I am defining treatable sex offenders as those who are judged to be *psychopathic* rather than *psychotic*. Most experts seem to agree that the majority of sex offenders are psychopathic.

A psychopath, according to Arthur Teicher et al., learns to respond to situations in devious ways because normal responses fail to win him respect. He characteristically has a history of lifelong difficulties, including rages, frustrations, and pent-up emotions. These feelings usually result from extreme sibling rivalry, lack of familial love, and extreme conflict between the parents of the offender themselves. The psychopath becomes lost in the struggle and powerless to change the situation in which he finds himself.[6]

Once a psychopathic condition has been established, it forms a self-reinforcing, self-defeating cycle. A psychopathic person learns to replace a painful condition with one more acceptable to him; these replacements become more and more necessary, often taking the form of fantasy. For instance, a young man for various reasons may question his masculinity, and is therefore unable to associate normally with women. As a result, he may become obsessed with curiosity about female sex organs. His initial outlet may be window-peeping (voyeurism). In his effort to prove his manhood, he may show his penis to women (exhibitionism). He seems to be saying, "Look, I have one too; I'm really a man!"

Constant masturbation with the fantasy of sexual intercourse may accompany his activities. Occasional fantasizing is normal; behavior becomes "deviant" when it is obsessive, antisocial, or aggressive. If ultimately these fantasies do not contain a psychopath's anger and frustration, rape is frequently the next step; he does get temporary relief from these behaviors. Eventually this person believes that living is not possible without these substitutes (deviant behaviors).

The psychopath experiences no loss of contact with

reality, however; [although he may not act rationally or in accordance with behavior that is socially acceptable, he can at least appreciate the difference. The psychotic, on the other hand, loses all contact with reality.] He retreats into a world of his own to which penetration from the outside is difficult, if not impossible. Most therapists believe that the psychotic is not amenable to help.

The following case history is a classic example of a life destined to be psychopathic and, in this instance, sexually psychopathic. Lawrence is a thirty-one-year-old rapist whom I met at a maximum-security treatment center.

"I was born a bastard," he said. "The thought even to this day gives me a bad taste. My mom tried to get rid of me at seven months—unfortunately I was born. She left me in the hospital, but my grandparents (they were her parents) took me out." Lawrence does not know why, but at age six he went to live with his mother for three months—the first time he knew of her existence. During his stay, his stepfather and some friends, who had been drinking heavily, forced the boy to perform fellatio. Terrified, he finally broke away and ran to his mother. "I was crying, naturally, and scared to death. I wasn't really sure what they'd done to me. My mom smacked me around, told me to stop acting like a big baby and then made me come down on her. I ran outside and stayed in a field all night. I had to live with my mother for three shitty months, and then I went back to my grandparents."

This period of Lawrence's life was so repugnant that only after many months of therapy did he recall the experience. It had been blocked completely from his memory.

When Lawrence was ten years old, his grandmother, who he then believed was his mother, died. The boy took her death as a personal rejection. His grandfather explained what their true relationship was, and Lawrence could not understand the lie. His grandparents, who were strictly religious, had taught him that honesty was a cardinal virtue.

He felt betrayed, and spent much time thereafter with a group of older boys, smoking and occasionally drinking on the sly.

At age thirteen, Lawrence became too difficult for his grandfather to handle, so back he went to his mother. He did not remember ever having lived there before. His mother and her family ignored him. "I felt completely outside—no one accepted me." After six months, he ran away, started stealing cars and generally misbehaving. From then on, most of his life was spent in penal institutions. Until age twenty-three, his repeated crime was robbery.

Lawrence always had been aware of what he called an "effeminate" side of his personality—a side that wanted to serve and comfort people. Working as an aide in a hospital supported him financially, and also helped satisfy this urge to serve. But he considered wanting to be kind and friendly a weakness, and he tried to keep this aspect of his character hidden. "I really hated fighting and all that crap, but in my world there wasn't no other way."

When Lawrence was in his late twenties, he started living with a woman whom he grew to care for. He bought her clothes and even did the cooking. He enjoyed the life, but at the same time he was ashamed of it. "I was fulfilling my effeminate side through her." One evening, in the apartment elevator, after they had been out having a beer, he knocked his girl friend down and raped her. Grabbing her by the hair, he then pulled her into a public toilet and raped her again. "What I see about the whole situation was that I was attacking my feminine self—I was trying to destroy it."

After the incident was over, he took the woman to a hospital, went back to the apartment, found a shotgun, but could not get the courage to kill himself. The rape was not reported, much to his surprise. From then on, he lived two separate lives—working in the hospital by day, and raping women at night. His victims were residents of his neighborhood whom he knew only by sight. He explained, "It's a funny thing. They were always the friendly ones. They might say, 'Good evening' or 'Hi,' and that made me feel like hurting them—raping them. I couldn't stand nice women." He was eventually caught, and now who knows what his future for rehabilitation is.

Psychopathic behavior may result from more than a psychological cause. Recently it was discovered that an abnormality of the sex chromosomes appears to create psychopathy in the absence of any environmental cause. Dr. Robert Deisher, who heads the Juvenile Sex Offender Program in Seattle, Washington, has reported some of these findings. His samplings are as yet too small for conclusive data.[7] Dr. Nelson Handler of Johns Hopkins Hospital discovered a type of temporal epilepsy that seems to cause sexual psychopathology. In some of these cases, the application of drugs or brain surgery removed the symptoms. Again, the cases found were few.[8] At any rate, it appears that only an extremely small number of psychopaths, by any definition, show these physical abnormalities.

One recurring theme in the life history of psychopaths is a completely disordered early environment. The extent of the chaos varies from case to case, and it is puzzling to note that some children can experience the most disturbed and disorganized home situation without developing any apparent psychopathic disorder in later life. Here, as elsewhere in practical psychology research, usually only one member in a chaotic family of several children will become psychopathic. (During my travels, I only once found two sex offenders in a family.) Perhaps individual heredity is important in determining who does and who does not succumb to a disruptive early environment. If we look into our own families, we can see this difference, too.

One of the founders of the Treatment Center for Sexual Offenders at Western State Hospital, Robinson Williams, explained the effect of early environment on sexual psychopaths. "When you read dozens and dozens of life histories, the theme is almost universally of deprivation in their earliest years. Their families are disrupted in one way or another by a father whom they never knew, and a mother who was bitter toward the father. Constant fighting—sometimes viciously violent—is common in their homes. A lack of responsibility on the part of the mother who may be mentally ill, alcoholic, or promiscuous. The children learn to distrust rather than be emotionally dependent on the parent figure. There is a lack of teaching civilized values, such as sharing and consideration for other members of the family. They may be told what not to do without the carrier wave of love and true concern. The behavior then becomes a punishing and critical thing only.

"Through these values, they learn that the world is a hard, cruel, and unloving place where you cannot trust people. They are taught this early in life. They have an education in distrust and 'lonerism.' They keep everything to themselves —their feelings and thoughts. Who do you talk to if no one gives a damn? And thus the pattern of dwelling in compensatory fantasy becomes the only sure way that they can fulfill whatever needs they have, sexual and otherwise. They can make up images in a dream world which is not shared, talked over, or revealed to any other human being. That little world becomes like a locked cell."

Psychopaths are often unable to handle frustration, and are unreliable. Impulsiveness and disregard for the results of their actions are other common characteristics. Such behavior is usual in children. Most psychopaths fail to mature emotionally. According to P. J. Gebhard and his associates, "The childhood of a patterned sex offender is one of emotional difficulties coupled with sexual activity. His adult life consists of a conflicting mixture of restraints, desires, and worries. These are associated with or caused by an unusual interest in experimenting with unconventional sexual activities."[9] This statement describes sex offenders as guilt-ridden persons in conflict over their sexuality, and therefore somewhat obsessed (in an inhibited way) with sex.

But again, we should not be confused by the popular stereotype of the sex offender as a totally unstable sex-obsessed maniac whose wild imagination can easily cause uncontrollable sexual acts.

Dr. Ian Macindoe, who was one of the first to experiment with sex-offender treatment in Minnesota, believes that the majority of sex offenders are the kind of people you meet every day as you walk down the street; that many rapists, for example, are otherwise seemingly ordinary men who have a particular problem in handling their aggressions, their hostilities, and their resentments. These weaknesses result in sexual assaults.

I have observed that psychopaths can be very charming, making immediate social contact easy. (At one of the treatment programs I visited, I mistook a rapist for a therapist.) The charm, however, is only superficial—psychopathic personalities are incapable of forming deep, meaningful relationships. They are often described as feeling no love or affection, and having little concern for others. It is not surprising to find that the social and sexual life of the psychopath is chaotic and shallow.

As Robinson Williams pointed out, "Some sex offenders are even 'glad-handers' on the surface, and may superficially have many friends, but no real ones. They may lie beside their wives in bed, have children by them, but still not reveal their inner selves. Like many people, they marry to satisfy their sexual appetites, often on an extremely hasty basis without really knowing the woman."

The emotionally underdeveloped man who is unconsciously looking for a mother will often find someone who is seeking a permanent child—one who will not grow up and leave her. "More than the ordinary young man, they [sex offenders] are dependent emotionally," continued Williams. "Not having matured in that area, they are still children looking for a mother. Often their wives are maneuvered into being mothers—handling the finances and making all the household decisions. Their wives are many times manipulated into what I call a 'bitch mother'—one who is forced into a position of saying 'no' to them frequently. The sex-offender husband, through her, finds a justification for being even more irresponsible. He then complains that his wife is unsympathetic and unloving—and thus the vicious cycle continues. Like most of the characteristics of sex offenders, these complaints are not too different from those of many men who marry. The psychopath carries them to an extreme."

When such a marriage occurs, both the husband and wife have warped ideas and feelings about their responsibilities. It becomes obvious that, although many sex offenders marry, their marriages are usually disastrous. Where children result, the cycle often is repeated in their own lives.

Children are so deeply involved in the psychological attitudes of their parents that it is no wonder that most of their nervous disturbances can be traced to an agitated atmosphere in the home. The essential fact behind all this is that behavior that has the most powerful effect upon children does not come from their parents' conscious state but from their unconscious motivation. Of course, our parents were themselves born of humans and not of the gods. They too had to face the handicap of their environment and heritage. The errors for which they are now blamed were not necessarily of their own making. In order to break the cycle, each generation must assume the responsibility for its own behavior instead of excusing it in the guise of family background.

Like Frances Wilckes, I have long believed that the Golden Rule as stated in the Bible is fallacious. In attempting to understand human beings in general and sex offenders in particular, it should be changed to read: "Do unto others as you would have them do *if you were they.*"[10] How can we possibly follow this rule so interpreted without an understanding of what our brother or sister really is and how he or she differs from us? We must realize that this difference will continue until the end of time.

# 2

# The Chaotic Lives of Sex Offenders

The following stories of sex offenders dramatically illustrate some of the environmental and psychological factors that influence deviant behavior. One or more of these factors were found to some extent in the lives of all of the sex offenders I interviewed.

Louis is an intelligent, warm, attractive young man. He is serving a long sentence for aggravated rape at a state prison. The prison in which he is confined is sixty-five years old. It fits the stereotype of a steel fortress that warehouses men in crowded cages piled one on top of the other, reaching to the ceiling. The decor is stark, bilious yellow tile. The hard surface adds to the din of the clanging hardware. The small town in which the prison is located is quiet and idyllic. Trees line the streets, which are decorated with old, stately houses. The prison is well hidden at the outskirts so that residents of the town can easily ignore its ugliness.

One hot summer evening, when the temperature and humidity outside had risen to ninety degrees, I met with Louis in a prison room. The thermometer there must have registered one hundred degrees. There was no movement of air. From the stagnant room, I had a clear view of other men moving at a languid pace, up and down, up and down the hall. They resembled animals confined in a poorly designed zoo. They were mopping their bodies with towels.

The normally violent prison atmosphere is aggravated by summer heat. When temperatures rise, so do tempers. Blood often flows as the men express their frustrations. They lash out at each other with any available instrument. Louis described the penitentiary as an incessant battlefield. The sight of blood was commonplace, he told me. He was now quite immune to it.

While Louis was telling his story, I was struck by how articulate and self-analytical he was. He seemed to know exactly what had caused him to commit sexual offenses and obviously had spent a great deal of time thinking about it. He said that he had had a rather happy childhood until he was about seven years old and his parents were divorced. He then didn't see his father until he was twelve.

"I was a problem child," Louis said, "but not really delinquent. I never got to school on time or told my mother where I was going, or where I had been. I thought my mother did not care about what I was doing, but I now think she felt guilty because of the divorce that took away my father. As a result, she didn't discipline me the way she should have. I subconsciously resented her and this may have been the beginning of my poor self-image and my resentment of women.

"My father was an alcoholic and at the time I went to live with him when I was twelve, he was drinking heavily. He wanted me to live with him because he was lonesome. I think my mother was really glad to get rid of me. Of course, my dad was in no position to rear a child who was coming into his teens. I ended up doing a lot of 'babysitting' for him over the next four or five years. I even had to put him in jail sometimes. Whenever he would begin to drink, my stepmother and I would more or less take turns watching him. We tried to keep him from getting out to buy a bottle."

When Louis first moved in with his father, his stepmother was not drinking, but over the years she also became an alcoholic. In 1970 she died, either by freezing to death or from acute alcoholism: she had been gone for five days when they found her frozen in the front seat of her car in a parking lot.

"I started drinking quite heavily when I was sixteen. I just got tired of having no life of my own," he said. "I saw no way out of it, really. You know, it's a funny thing, but the thought of running away never occurred to me. I loved my father but also resented him for not giving me the space I needed to form my own relationships."

Louis said that he thought he had accomplished nothing worthwhile in his life. He had not graduated from high school; not because he did not have the intelligence, but because he was hardly ever there. At thirteen, when he first went to court for truancy, he was put on probation. He had missed thirty or forty days of school.

Louis met his wife, Susan, when they were fourteen, and from that time on until they were married at eighteen, he dated few other girls. He spoke of his marriage. "Communicating was always difficult for us, but I thought that the marriage in general was satisfactory for her. It wasn't for me. I was looking for more excitement in our sex life. Throughout our marriage, I continued with the same lying pattern I had followed when I was young. I never admitted to doing wrong and was always on the defensive. I was afraid of losing her. It seems ironic to me now when I think how loyal she's been during all this trouble."

Susan was born into a religious family where drinking and smoking were prohibited. Louis agreed to give up alcohol and cigarettes after he and Susan were married, but he just was not ready. "So there I was," Louis said, "the first six years of my marriage, sneaking cigarettes and sneaking a drink. I thought, 'Well, what the hell's the matter with me? I'm afraid to tell my wife that I'm going to smoke in my own home, that I'm going to have a six-pack of beer in the refrigerator if I want it. If she doesn't like it, if she doesn't learn to adjust, we'll have to figure something else out.' Feelings don't go away by sitting on them and they weren't being faced up to. I wasn't aware of feeling resentful toward women; it just built up over the years. It was like a steam kettle or a pressure cooker. Finally it had to blow off.

"At the time of the first rape, there was a lot of pressure in just about every aspect of my life. I hated my job and was disgusted with myself. I felt worthless. Making payments on a fifty-thousand-dollar home and a new car was a struggle. My wife and I were caught up in a status thing."

Louis expressed how he felt after the first rape: "I was sure that I wouldn't ever do it again. I had no idea what had gotten into me. I couldn't understand it and I certainly could not share it with my wife. I could share it with no one at all. Who could I contact—and talk to? I just had no direction. I had no idea what was going on. When I got home that night, I acted pretty much normal, as though nothing had happened. I was quite nervous but covered it up with some excuse. It was the pattern of our relationship, anyway—our lack of communication."

Most of the sex offenders I talked with shared many of the experiences and characteristics Louis had: a chaotic early environment in which their parents quarreled excessively or were alcoholic; a low self-image; the inability to communicate with those closest to them—parent or spouse. Richard, a twenty-four-year-old multiple rapist, told me that he came from "a wandering kind of family. We lived in twenty-six houses in almost as many cities by the time I was thirteen." His father held a variety of short-lived jobs; his mother worked when the family needed extra money. "I communicated very little with my mother," Richard said, "and when we did talk, it was always about impersonal subjects. The first time I ever talked to her for more than ten minutes about anything more serious than the weather, or what my brothers were doing, was when she visited me in prison."

It was clear that Richard, like Louis, had given much thought to what had influenced his behavior: "After I was four or five years old, my parents gave me no demonstrative affection. The neighborhoods we lived in varied depending on the income. Some were rough, where the kids traveled in gangs, and others had more stable families. We moved so often that close friends were scarce, and coupled with a lack of family warmth, I felt isolated. One of my brothers who had had polio when he was six got most of the attention, I thought, and this added to my feelings of neglect. The only time I got any notice from either of my parents was when I did well in athletics. There was too much emphasis on winning and excelling; it made me too aggressive."

As an adolescent, Richard became involved in some window-peeping behavior. He started to commit the rapes after serving in the military. Adjusting to civilian life was difficult, and the world seemed hostile. He said, "In raping, there was a kind of chase and conquest that gave me a sort of satisfaction."

The serious sibling rivalry that Richard experienced and the competition for parental affection were common to many of the offenders I interviewed. A large number felt no love or respect from their parents.

Both Joey and Tom, two juvenile child molesters, showed some of the same characteristics. A conversation with Joey's father revealed a low opinion of his son: "He's shy and clumsy. He's not very bright either. My other three kids always done a lot better in school. The girls don't like him very much either. But I'm bringing him up to be a good

Christian." He explained that he had taught Joey that masturbation is a sin. "It softens the brain," he contended.

Joey was an attractive young man whose fluffy blond hair hung to his shoulders. He was sixteen years old. Of his father he said, "He's awful strict and thinks I'm dumb. I guess I am, all right, not as bright as the rest of them. He don't think I do nothing right." He admitted to being afraid of girls, and said he seemed to fall over his feet whenever he was near them. "I don't know how to talk to them. I'm too shy, and they don't pay no attention to me." He drew pictures of houses for recreation.

Both Joey and his father referred to his mother, who had been ill for several years. Said the father, from whom she was divorced: "We don't want to be seen in public with her. She's beginning to look like her inner attitude—ugly, hateful, mean, nasty, and impolite." He later told me that she had contracted Huntington's chorea before Joey was born, but he seemed to know little about the nature of the disease. (The medical dictionary states that it is a genetic, progressive, muscular degeneration of the body and brain leading to complete immobility and idiocy.)

After the divorce the children lived with their mother for a few years. The father said that she spent most of the day on the davenport, drunk; when the children complained, she would beat them. Joey confirmed the beatings and added: "She was sick all the time with some bad disease. I don't know what it is. She got mad at us easy, and hit us with a strap."

Joey's description of what happened between him and the little girl he molested illustrates his gross lack of sexual information: "I only wanted to look at her and feel her to see what girls were like. I didn't mean to hurt her, so I didn't think it was wrong. All I did was to stick my finger in her hole a couple of times. I guess I must have hurt her though because she yelled when her mother washed her. That's how what I did was found out."

Tom was also sixteen and, like Joey, was afraid of girls. He experienced intense sibling rivalry; he felt unable to measure up to his younger brother, whose athletic ability was admired by the father. He too preferred to spend his leisure time drawing. Tom described his problems: "All my life, my father was at me to be like my little brother. He's good at sports. I'm not. I try to be, but I always mess it up. The other kids make fun of me and my dad tells me that I don't do a single thing right. I'm afraid of girls. I tried talking to one once, and she just walked away.

"Then one evening when I was babysitting with a neighborhood girl and her brother, the girl went to the bathroom. I think she called me—anyhow, I went in just as she was getting off the toilet seat. For some reason, I all of a sudden went in and stuck my finger up her pee hole. I don't know why, but after she went to bed, I went in her room and 'jerked off' on her. Her brother was in the next room. I went in there and made him suck me. I don't know why I did these things. I don't really remember doing them. They say I did, so I guess they're right. The kids told their mother a few days later and she called the police."

Tom's therapist said that when Tom first came to the clinic he had blotted the incident out of his mind. As I talked to Tom, he seemed unsure whether what he was saying came from memory or from what he was told. According to the therapist, the temporary erasure of traumatic acts is not unusual. He further said that Tom was in such a depressed state when they originally talked that the boy had attempted suicide.

Joey and Tom became sex offenders at a very early age, but this is not surprising. Amir's Philadelphia research revealed that many sex offenders who had an arrest record as adults also had a record of sexual offenses as juveniles.[1]

Bernie, a nineteen-year-old rapist, started committing sex offenses at a young age. He told me that he came from a family that was dominated by his father—a very handsome and self-confident man. For the most part, the father ignored his children (three boys and two girls), but would, on occasion, try to win their favor by buying them ice cream and candy. The boy's mother was treated as an inferior. Frequently the father would leave the house late at night, and return in the morning. The boy thought his father was with other women, and his mother confirmed his suspicions.

Like Joey and Tom, Bernie felt inferior to his siblings, who ignored him. He joined a rowdy group of boys, and took part in their shoplifting activities because it made him feel important. He became obsessed with curiosity about sex, but was too shy to be with girls. At sixteen, he started window-peeping, exposing, drinking heavily, and stealing girls' underwear.

One evening, while drunk, Bernie broke into the home of a family friend, intending to rape her. She was out. In his stupor, he removed his clothes in preparation for the rape and waited for her. She returned and of course discovered him. After his arrest, Bernie was sent to a sex-offender therapeutic community center, where he is undergoing treatment.

It is well known that American culture, despite changes that have occurred in recent years, is still one of the most sexually puritanical, immature, and ignorant societies in the Western world. A large proportion of sex offenders know nothing of even the simplest facts about sexual responses. Their obsessive curiosity about sex certainly is understandable.

According to Frances Wilckes, the greatest wrong that the early Christian church did to humanity was to separate the body from the spirit, labeling one base and the other holy. If guilt is attached to sexual feelings, the child who masturbates perceives himself as isolated by his unforgivable sin. A sense of inferiority separates him from others and he is driven into a fantasy world. With each return to masturbation, the sense of guilt deepens and so a vicious cycle is formed.[2] I found this pattern repeated in the lives of many sex offenders. A lack of sex education along with a strict negative religious upbringing, e.g., homosexuality and masturbation are *sinful,* are common characteristics in the family training of sex offenders.

Maurice, a thirty-year-old rapist, began his sexual offenses by exhibitionism. His story illustrates how an unhealthy attitude toward sex and religion can seriously distort a life. He was one of the few offenders I met to have had a homosexual experience. (Most offenders in treatment programs are heterosexual, though they may have had occasional homosexual relations that were nonviolent sexual contacts.) He is also the only offender I met whose brother was sexually deviant. He has been in treatment for four years, and is thankful to be there instead of prison.

Maurice told me that when he was growing up he had almost nothing to do with his father, who was "always working." His mother was at home but Maurice felt that she was preoccupied with his baby brother. "I wanted to be close to my father—to do things with him, to be loved and to feel like I belonged. Now that I look back on my parents, I can see that they really loved me but didn't take time to show it."

Maurice started exposing when he was thirteen, and that, he claimed, led to rape. "I went to a Catholic school," he said, "where the boys and girls were separated. We were taught that sex was dirty. Being with girls made me feel awkward and clumsy. I was really 'into the church' at that time; I even thought of becoming a priest.

"About then, I also had a homosexual experience with an older man. Almost before I knew it, I was wrapped up in his world, which gave me mixed feelings. There was shame, but also a certain pleasure. I was afraid to go to my parents because of what they would think of me. Having been brought up to believe that homosexuality was a sin, I felt down on me, but held the feeling inside. But it came out in different ways. I exposed more, rebelled against school, my parents, and everybody. You see, I was trying to suppress the demons inside of me. The church taught me that masturbation was a sin, too. It seemed that all of my natural feelings were sinful, and I felt very low."

When Maurice was in his early twenties he got picked up for indecent exposure. This was the first time his parents realized that anything was wrong. "They wanted to send me to a psychiatrist, but I was afraid to go. While I was on probation, I decided to get married as a solution to my problems. Of course, it only made them worse. I wanted to be married and still to run around as well. My wife knew I'd been arrested and used to tell me, 'If you feel like there's anything wrong, come and tell me.' But I didn't want to talk about my problems; I was too ashamed. So when I did get arrested for attempted rape, my wife left me. I really didn't blame her.

"For eleven months, I was in jail awaiting trial. Since I had previously dated my victim, the state decided that they had a weak case, so they got me to cop the plea to assault. I was sent to a psychiatrist, but he just asked me a few questions and told me I didn't need to come back. At that point, I really wanted to talk to somebody, but this guy didn't care."

When Maurice was released from jail, he and his wife reconciled. But around that time his brother, who had been arrested for indecent exposure, committed suicide in jail. "Things blew up," he said. "I was drinking a lot. I totally gave up on myself and tried to commit suicide by crashing my car. A woman stopped to help me. I pushed her by the side of the road and raped her. After that I was paroled to this program, and it has helped me a lot. I'm trying to get an insight as to where I'm at. If I'd gone to prison, I'd have come out the same as I went in or worse."

In our sexist society, men are expected to be superior to women in almost every respect. They are supposed to be physically stronger, emotionally more stable—even stoic—and at the same time, sexually adequate, even irresistible. Many men find this image impossible to fulfill, but feel pressured to assume a posture of self-confidence. Perhaps the most dominant of these demands is for the proof of masculine adequacy. Most men who doubt their own masculinity experience the greatest humiliation.

Barry was a puppeteer in his thirties who was arrested after attempting to molest a twelve-year-old girl. The court gave him the choice of probation with no treatment or commitment to a mental hospital where there was therapy. He chose the latter. "Of course I didn't like the idea of being locked up," he admitted to me, "but I knew my sex problems were getting serious, so I decided on the hospital treatment."

Barry described some of the causes of his problems. "My wife was not from a show business background. I guess you have to be somebody who understands this business to really know what it's all about—it's not for everyone. We got into a bad financial situation because I had to go on the road to make my living and my wife didn't want to join me. So I tried to find work in our home town to please her. After a while, I was climbing the walls because I wasn't working in my profession. So there was friction—a lot of it. Then we got into some pretty bad sexual problems. My wife had pretty kinky hangups on sex. She would use it to get her way. I was made to feel very much less than a man. I didn't handle it right, I guess—anyway it went from bad to worse. It got to the point where sex was a bad word to her.

"She finally went on the road with me but we were always fighting. When we got home, the bills had piled up and our sex life hadn't changed. I was terribly depressed and felt that I'd failed us both. What was happening to my manhood bothered me. Then I got arrested for indecent exposure. I knew that my wife and I should have some help, but we didn't know where to go."

Barry finally got offered a job that looked promising, and it was planned that his wife and their child would join him later. But when he started the job, he found the housing situation intolerable and the job misrepresented. "I just didn't give a shit about anything," he confessed. "Quite honestly, I was ready for sex. I wrote an extremely obscene note to a young girl. She was thirteen years old and they told me she was the town whore. To show you how nervous I was, I gave it to the wrong girl. Well, that of course did it. There was a trial for attempting to seduce a minor. The judge sent me to the state hospital for a month. I talked to a psychiatrist about my marriage troubles and he decided that my deep depression was the cause. I was released on probation and had no sex offenses during that year.

"Shortly after, my wife filed divorce papers and I felt bitter. From then on, I had complete distrust for women. I was scared as hell to even attempt a date with a mature woman. I didn't want to get hurt again. My thinking and fantasizing centered on young girls. They wouldn't hurt me, I thought. Then I was arrested again—this time for molesting a young girl and after that I committed myself to the hospital."

Barry's need to dominate and control women—to prove his virility—was shared by many of the offenders I met. Their feelings of low self-esteem seemed to be linked with a lack of confidence in their maleness. Again, it is clear that sex offenders differ from the rest of us only in degrees.

Luke, a twenty-year-old rapist, is in his second year of therapy. He can intellectualize his guilt but still cannot feel it and will have to remain in treatment until he overcomes this character flaw. His experiences illustrate how the shallowness of relationships can stem from a need to dominate.

Luke was raised in a rigid Roman Catholic household. He told me that he hated his mother "because she controlled both my dad and me. Not only did my mother tell us what to do, but we were supposed to enjoy what we were doing, and say so." In line with his strict religious upbringing, he had been taught to believe that masturbation was sinful. "I masturbated, but felt dirty doing it—worse than when I forced sex."

When he was about ten years old, Luke began fantasizing about sex as devious and hurtful. At sixteen, he had his first experience with sex, which he forced on the girl. The pleasure he got was in the feeling of control. "The love I had for the girls was what they could do for me," he confessed. "Women were objects for my pleasure."

Luke was considered to be outgoing. Speech was one of his favorite subjects, and the girls found him attractive. Because he knew that his speeches were a cover-up for his own feelings of inferiority, and that he used women as a shield for his sexual inadequacy, Luke developed self-hatred. "No one could ever get close to me. I was always on my guard."

Most of his rapes were performed on dates, and he could rationalize that the girls really wanted it. The last two, for which he was charged, were with strangers. "I didn't physically injure them. The first rape happened when the woman was walking down the street late one night. I came up behind her, started a conversation, then I put her in a choke hold—pushed her down a flight of stairs, and then raped her. I got into the parked car of the second woman. I hid in the back seat until she came back and had driven a few blocks, then I leaped over the seat, threatened her and then raped her."

*

George, another rapist, also told me of his need to strike out at women—to denigrate them. The treatment center to which he was sent is located in a state with a large black population, and in the prison I visited, 95 percent of the inmates were black. I observed relatively few blacks in this treatment center, however. After voicing this observation to George, he explained that most whites think black women welcome sexual acts and cannot be raped. Therefore, few men, black or white, are convicted for raping black women. Contrary to popular belief, Amir found that the majority of sex offenses are intraracial rather than interracial; that is, black and black, white and white.[3]

George's father, whom he admired deeply, had died of a heart attack at the young age of twenty-nine. He had owned a fleet of taxicabs and was considered to be a successful businessman. But when he died, the large hospital bill left the family of six children with almost no money, making it necessary for George's mother to be employed full time. Since she had little education or occupational skill, she worked in a laundry. Because George was the eldest son, he was expected to assume the role of his father—a position that made him uncomfortable and resentful. He resented the fact that his mother could not get a better job, and decided that the reasons were both her sex and her skin color. His anger at white women, he feels, stemmed from that belief.

School work came easily for George's sister, who was a year older, and the teachers continually compared his ability, which was only average, to his sister's. This situation just added to his other frustrations.

After his father's death, George started acting up by joining a gang of rough boys. There he felt a part of a group, and adequate to their expectations. They were curious about sex and did some window-peeping and flashing, but never got caught.

George's schooling ended at the eleventh grade, and he joined the army. The lack of respect for women and blacks that he experienced in the service made him even more hateful of himself and women. He raped many white women after returning home, but was caught only the last time. In thinking about his mother now, he has sympathy for her having to work all day and then dividing her time at home six ways. There are portions of his life that he has blotted out, and he is in the process of trying to uncover them.

The story of another sex offender, Bill, vividly portrays the importance of early detection and treatment of offenders. Like most of the cases I came across, the potential Bill had for serious sexual abuse was apparent quite early. His family knew he had a fetish for stealing women's underwear, but chose to ignore it. His parents, who were alcoholics, fought constantly as he was growing up. The children often had to call for help in separating them. As a result, Bill and his siblings spent as much time as possible away from home.

"Both my brother and I were troublemakers in grade school, but my brother didn't have any sexual problems. I started stealing my sister's underwear when I was ten. I remember once I had taken a bath, and had stuffed a pair of her panties in my crotch. As I came out of the bathroom, they fell out of my pajama leg. My father was there and he asked about it but never did anything else. Later on I took my mother's underwear, too. The whole family knew what I was doing, but they just ignored it. Everyone was too embarrassed to bring the subject up," Bill said. "None of my friends knew."

Later he stole underwear from his sister's friends whom he thought attractive. "I would masturbate in them, and fantasize about the girls. I had some girl friends, but my sex life came from masturbation. I had a hard time even kissing girls. I trace that back to one time when I was in the first or second grade, and a girl slapped me when I tried to kiss her." That fear even carries over now to his relationship with the woman he is presently dating. "I've always been afraid I might be rejected," he said.

As a teenager, Bill spent much of his time after school and on weekends with a group of boys who congregated outside the corner drugstore. "We drank beer and smoked and bribed winos to buy the beer. My first experience with real sex was when I and these boys passed a girl around—kind of group sex. She was in the neighborhood and willing to do it. It wasn't fun for me; it was ugly."

During this period of his life, he went out with only one girl. He thought he loved her, but they didn't have sexual relations. He stole her underwear, too.

When Bill was sixteen, he started window-peeping, and stealing underwear from the girls he was watching. He hid the clothing in his closet. When he was seventeen, he was seen stealing clothes off the line in an apartment house, and the police caught him. He said: "Until then, I didn't see what I was doing as all that bad. I thought I could stop any time I wanted to."

Bill was put on probation, and his family concocted a story to explain the reason. A psychiatrist met with him every week for a year. "The man turned out to be homosexual and treated me as if I was a homosexual, too. His therapy was to have me pull down my pants, and then he would touch my sex organs. I was told to get together with my friends and to look at their penises." Although Bill questioned this procedure, he did not complain. Getting off probation was all important. His fetish was never discussed by the psychiatrist. "I didn't want to talk about it anyway; the whole hour was a bunch of bullshit. After the year was up, I was told I was cured. I had learned to be more careful about where I stole the underwear," he said.

Bill's fetish continued and he finally began to realize that he did have a problem. About then he began buying pornographic magazines; his fantasies included some of what he saw. Bill spent two years as a soldier, in Vietnam, where he continued his fetish, using underwear he had brought with him. His girl friend and her family knew nothing of his problems and so made plans for their marriage. "After five years of dating, I married my girl friend," he said. "I certainly wasn't ready for marriage, but didn't know how to get out of it."

His wife, Beatrice, he described as "outgoing and very grown-up—not like me. When we were first married she went to school while I worked moving furniture and going to the university at night. My job was boring and I was always griping. After Beatrice graduated and got a job, she told me to quit and go to school full time. By then what I wanted was more money so we could buy a home and a car. Another reason was that our working hours gave me the time for pornographic movies and stealing underwear. My wife worked from three o'clock to eleven, and I got home at five o'clock, so I had several free hours. I thought being married would change me, but it didn't."

Their life was complicated by other difficulties. Bill continued to meet with his old group of friends, have parties, and get drunk. His wife was a social drinker, but disliked the kind of parties he enjoyed. All the men gathered together on one side of the room and got drunk, leaving the women alone. There was much arguing and his wife became less and less interested in joining him on those occasions. He was jealous of her, too. She had a job that was challenging, while he was just floundering. Beatrice's whole family was school-oriented; all of them had college degrees. They continually pressed him to finish college, but he felt insecure about his ability to do so.

"By then, we owned a house and two cars," Bill explained. "I had stolen clothing in the trunk of my car, so I kept the keys to both trunks. I felt very guilty, but I couldn't face up to telling my wife. Our sex life was not good. Sometimes we went for three or four weeks without sexual intercourse. I still masturbated and went to the movies."

After five years of marriage, his wife became pregnant. A friend told him that women in that condition were sexually repulsive, and that was the way he related to her. Finally they had no sexual relations at all. He committed his first rape at this time. "It was after I had been to a porn movie and as usual I felt horny. I drove to a house where I knew a woman lived and looked in a window to see if she was there. I intended to steal her underwear. This time when I saw her, instead of just looking, I went in and raped her. After that, I felt so sick I thought I'd never do it again."

After the baby was born, Bill was sure he would straighten out, but he didn't. At the second attempted rape, the woman screamed, and he ran away in fright. After reading an article in a magazine stating that women were less resistant to a weapon, he decided to carry a knife. "I was scared to death every time, but when I showed the knife, the women didn't struggle any more. It was only a threat. I don't think I ever would have used it." All of his victims were strangers.

His wife finally learned about his fetish. "One night on my way home from work, I stole some underwear off a line, went to bed, started masturbating, and fell asleep. When my wife got home, there I was. I made some lame explanation that I know she didn't believe, but she didn't say anything. The last few months before I was arrested, I couldn't sleep much, so I think Beatrice knew something was wrong," he said.

Bill told me about his last rape. "I was coming home from work when a woman turned in front of me. She lived just two blocks from my home, and I'd noticed her before. My wife and I had been invited to a party that night, and she refused to go because she knew there would be a lot of drinking. We had recently turned down three other similar invitations for the same reason, so this time I decided to go alone. When I left my house, I drove on the street where I had previously seen the woman. I had intended to break in and steal her underwear. When I looked in the window and she was there, I changed my mind, and decided to come back later after the party. I stayed at the party until midnight, and got pretty well plotched. When I got back to the woman's house, I still had it in mind to steal the underwear. But there she was, alone, and getting ready for bed. It took me until two A.M. to get enough courage to knock on the door. This was after she'd turned off the lights. When she came, I told her I was delivering a pizza, which of course she hadn't ordered. When she tried to close me out, I forced my way in by showing the knife. It had taken me so long to get the nerve to enter that I was uncontrollable. Nothing could have stopped me from going ahead. If she'd fought, it would have done her no good. She said that she was expecting her husband any minute, so I forced her out of the house and pushed her into my car. We drove a few blocks away, and I raped her in the car. I was really very vicious because of the state of mind I was in.

"The next night, I had an accident with my car after I'd been drinking. Just before that I'd tried to rape another woman but she got away. I was taken to the police station to be tested for how drunk I was. There were two sets of police involved—the ones in the attempted rape, and those at the accident. They were all at the police station when I was brought in. The officers who were called after the attack saw me, and thought I looked like the description of the attacker."

When the police presented his picture to the woman he had just attempted to rape, she identified him. The victim of the night before recognized his car. At first he pleaded not guilty, but the evidence was overwhelming, and he changed his mind.

He explained his feelings: "I felt both depressed and re-

lieved. I was sure my life had ended. I knew I would b
locked up for at least forty years. But there was a fantastic
amount of relief, too. I didn't have to pretend any more.
For the first time my wife knew that I was a rapist."

Bill was charged with rape and kidnaping. After two psychiatric examinations, he was sent to a mental hospital.
Both the psychiatrists and his attorney said that he needed
treatment desperately. It was arranged for him to be escorted to an out-patient clinic twice a week. Aversive conditioning, a much misunderstood and criticized therapy, was
effective in helping Bill overcome his fetish. (It is a specific
treatment for this kind of crime and is described more fully
in Chapter 5.) He lived at the hospital for three years, where
he experienced group therapy as well as counseling at the
treatment center. During the last year, he spent some weekends with his parents. Finally it was determined that he was
ready for release, but the kidnaping charge was still pend-
ing. This crime came under the jurisdiction of the department of correction, so his future was to be determined by
the parole board. The psychologist with whom he had
worked pleaded for his parole, arguing that imprisonment
would undo all positive effects of the treatment. They
finally agreed to his release; he was in prison only one day.

He is now living at home with his parents, and attending a
university. Once a week he sees a psychiatrist at the hospital
and according to his therapist, since Bill resisted growing up,
he is going through adolescence at age thirty. Sometimes his
parents join him in therapy but communication between
them is still difficult. They now know his problems should
have been faced when he was a child.


As we have seen, the lives of sex offenders are filled with
rage, frustration, and pent-up emotion. They learn to respond in devious ways because normal responses fail to win
respect. These feelings can result from poor self-image,
deprivation, extreme sibling rivalry, lack of love from their

families, a chaotic early environment, rigid religious instruction, inadequate sex education, and a fear of women that turns to hate. Sex offenders become lost in these struggles and become powerless to change the situation in which they find themselves.

The needs of sex offenders are the same as those of all humans: the love and respect of family and friends, a healthy attitude toward sex, a feeling of self-worth, and a responsible attitude toward their own behavior. They also need a consciousness of the immediate and future results of their actions, a respect for others regardless of sex or sexual preference, a recognition of their own limitations, and finally, a realization that all these requirements will never be completely satisfied.

# Part Two

# Can Therapy Help the Sex Offender?

# 3

# An Overview of Sex Offender Treatment Centers

What happens to the sex offender after he is convicted of a crime?

In most states a sex offender remains imprisoned for a maximum of five years (depending on the gravity of the crime). Without receiving any help, he is then released on parole and returned to the same community in which his problems occurred.

"Getting them off the streets" gives society a false sense of security, since prison is only a temporary holding force at best. Because the guards and other prisoners degrade him, the already low self-esteem of the sex offender drops even lower. He is often blamed for sexual attacks on other prisoners, and is himself considered a willing target for prison rape. Armed robbers and murderers are frequently admired for their courage and skill, and thereby gain a certain respect. Sex offenders, especially child molesters, are revered by no one.

Those committing lesser offenses, such as voyeurism or exhibitionism, are usually freed on probation with no attention given to their special problems. These misdemeanors indicate personality disorders that, left untreated, can lead to the commission of major crimes, as we have seen.

Can the incidence of sexual assault be reduced through therapeutic treatment? Recent statistics clearly point to the failure of our present system of punishment as a deterrent. According to the *United States Uniform Crime Reports* by the FBI, more than fifty-six thousand rapes were reported to the police in 1975. These figures represent a 41 percent increase in the rate of reported rapes from 1969 to 1975, making rape the fastest growing crime of violence among the four most frequent crimes: murder, aggravated assault, rape, and robbery.[1]

The American Correctional Association, organized over one hundred years ago by a group of prison reform advocates, became concerned with these figures and determined to find out what treatment was available nationwide for sex offenders. In 1976, the association appointed Edward Brecher, a writer in the field of human sexuality, as project director of a study entitled "Sex Offenders and Sex Offenses." The study was to be conducted nationally and its purpose was to develop a model sex-offender treatment program for use by systems which lack such a facility.[2]

Edward Brecher is one of the few people in the country with specific information about sex-offender treatment programs. When I met Brecher in April 1976, he had a list of twenty-four programs operating in the United States. These programs had several features in common. For one thing, they were all quite new. (Five years was considered to be a long-term program in this field.) They also were small in scale, with few inmates involved. (Most work specifically with the problems of parolees and probationers.) And none of them was well publicized. Officials in any one state were eager to learn what was happening elsewhere.

Most of the treatment programs Brecher studied are state-funded. Of course, they never have enough money. At least a dozen of the twenty-four treatment centers he identified are in state mental hospitals. As he pointed out, this is not accidental: "Over the past decade or more, the population of state mental hospitals has been going down almost everywhere, leaving vacant rooms, vacant floors and, in some places, vacant institutions. Mental hospitals as a whole, both maximum and minimum security systems, are included. However, most treatment centers are in security hospitals, but some have closed wards in open hospitals. Some institutions are thinking of other services they can render in the face of their declining population."

Brecher pointed out the economic benefits of placing treatment programs in state mental hospitals.

"Far from being a burden on the budget, it tends to be a form of saving. The difference in the guard system is part of the reason. To keep a man in a maximum security system costs more than sending him to Harvard. A guard for every two residents is usually needed, and sometimes even that isn't enough. Guards often earn $12,000 to $14,000 a year; thus you start with a $6,000 cost per year per man, not including room, board, treatment facilities, and psychiatric services.

"In a state hospital, the ratio of guards to offenders in a sex-offender unit is one in ten or twelve. Immediately you save $5,000 per man. Furthermore, if you compare these patients with those who are really sick and psychotic, with round-the-clock nursing and psychiatric intervention, the sex offender units tend to be almost self-supporting. The men are perfectly sane, willing and capable of taking on work assignments. In several hospitals, they're doing some of the best work and earning their keep very well. They are considered the cream of the crop."

An assistant county attorney I interviewed offered her criteria for a successful treatment program. In her opinion, there should be three kinds of facilities: a secure setting for those offenders who are violent and a particular danger to society; a less secure residential facility for those who are olent, either having left prison or having had therapy ... the secure setting; and finally, an outpatient program for those who are on probation or who have been previously treated. In this way the offenders gradually return to the community.

Brecher agreed: "A state should have a secure setting other than a prison for the treatment of a broad range of sex offenders. Equally important and simultaneously, there should be established a community program outside of the correctional system for offenders who do not need a secure setting and could therefore be safely treated in the community. If you don't have this community program at the same time, there will be two major difficulties. First, you will have no support group for the man who leaves the secure setting, and this makes no sense. Second, if you have a program in a secure setting which is the only one in your city, judges will inevitably send to that lockup men who could do equally well or better, and certainly be more economically treated, in the community."

He further said: "Suppose you have a program in your state hospital and one or more other programs. A substantial population of sex offenders will remain in the maximum security institutions with no help. As long as you have sex offenders in those institutions, there should be a program for them. It is sad but true that you cannot send all sex offenders, including multiple rapists with really vicious modes of behavior with respect to their victims, to a moderate security institution. Society won't tolerate it, and I'm not sure that we should. Very few sex offenders are included in this group. They are going to draw a long term in maximum security, but I don't think they should be forgotten. Perhaps they shouldn't be top priority, but a part of the threefold approach.

"In a well-designed institution where men need maximum security, they can be humanely treated if the situation is right and if you use well-tried techniques of security other than twenty-foot walls and guards."

This is outside his area of competence, Brecher admitted, but he believes that as long as we have our present system of long terms in maximum security, which he does not condone, we should at least afford some treatment services. Where there is a limited amount of money available for treatment of any kind, it should be put into the less secure settings, in his opinion. What is required for the large flow of sex offenders in the system is a moderately secure setting where the security does not get into the way of effective programming.

Brecher described several of the programs he has visited—among them, the program at the St. Cloud Reformatory in Minnesota. "Treatment is primarily for any chemically dependent inmates, a few of which are sex offenders. One of the influences is the enormous growth of help for drug-dependent persons. A large proportion of the new sex-offender programs are modeled on those drug programs, although the most common addiction for sex offenders is alcohol. The others seem to have a relatively small overlap. At St. Cloud they have no sex education, which makes the program less appropriate for sex offenders." Although it is entirely a drug addiction program, Brecher thinks that a similar one addressed specifically to sex problems could very well be established, using the same general pattern. Brecher visited several places where they did not separate sex offenders from other inmates. No such programs have impressed him favorably because they do not focus specifically on a man's sexual problems.

Some treatment centers he has seen support the premise that if a man can develop the skills to earn a living, and if he can learn to control his temper, then he has turned into a good citizen. Brecher is uncomfortable with this attitude. For unless the offender's sexual problems are dealt with, he is still a maladjusted person.

I asked Brecher who it is that determines whether or not a sex offender is ready to be released into the community.

"In most states," he explained, "the judge makes the ulti-

mate decision about when the men are ready for release."
There are great problems in this system, he believes. "When
a man has been living in an institution for two years under
close observation, and in close association with the other
members of his group, both they and the staff have a
pretty clear notion of what this person is like. They are able
to give their reports to the judge. However, the judge may
be two hundred miles away, and may have seen the man for
twenty minutes two or three years before, when he sentenced him. Fifteen or twenty minutes is all he usually takes
to reconsider the case. In my opinion, it is impossible for a
judge who handles a steady flow of criminal problems to do
the intensive assessment necessary to make an intelligent
decision about when a man is ready for release. In some
states the parole board is the final arbitrator, even though
the treatment program is in the hospital. It then is from the
corrections system that a man must be released," Brecher
explained.

I asked Brecher to comment on whether or not, in his
opinion, a therapist can be an objective judge of when an
offender he has treated is ready for release. In his eagerness
to have the program work, and with the desire of the offender to be free, would it not be possible for the therapist
to be overly optimistic and release him too early?

"There is that danger," Brecher agreed, "and there is
another consideration to which we should be equally sensitive. The staff, knowing that the program can be destroyed
if one man's escape happens to hit the front pages, may protect the program by holding the men too long. There are no
easy solutions. I personally have no recommendations.
However, I think it is terribly important that the views of
the therapists as well as those of the other men in the group
be given full consideration.

"What proportion of the graduates of the program live
successful, effective lives on the outside without re-
offending should be the ultimate grounds for evaluation. It

will be many years before we have reliable statistics, and we may never get them. If programs start playing the numbers game, showing how few of their offenders offend again, you get into terrible difficulties," Brecher warned. "First of all, a program can readily cut down the proportion of its offenders that re-offend by accepting only the easy, soft cases. Second, it can avoid graduating a man who represents even the slightest risk by sending him back to prison or giving him alternatives other than release with freedom. As a result, a program can get its re-offense rate down to zero, and be doing no good whatever. Looking at re-offense rates can be misleading."

Mr. Brecher has come to the conclusion that by observing the difference between the men who come in and those who go out, you very often can see an astonishing discrepancy.

"A man who comes in is clearly from the bottom of the barrel. He looks it, and he feels it. He is unable to cope with his own problems and those of living in the community. If an appreciable number of treated men show major changes by taking leadership and responsibility, there is real progress. We will have to assume that a man who goes out with his head up, competent, and with a greater understanding of himself and his problems is a better bet than the man who is released from prison without these changes. If he re-offends after having received treatment, he is rarely given an opportunity to return for additional therapy. The judge would be more likely to assume that the therapy had not done him any good. Long-term imprisonment would probably result. For parolees in general, a large number of parole violations for which a man is returned to prison are not criminal offenses. They are usually infractions of the parole provisions.

"It is very distressing to me that of the twenty-four programs there are in the country today, only two are in penal institutions. It appears that there is not much help there either. Men who are locked up for two, four, six, eight, or ten years can benefit from treatment. In the absence of a program, the likelihood of recidivism is high. In fact, offenders may come out more dangerous than when they entered. I am troubled because the correctional institutions have lagged so far behind other portions of the community in the area of treatment programs."

Brecher told me about some of the superior treatment programs he has visited. One that particularly impressed him was the program at Western State Hospital at Fort Steilacoom, Washington, which is discussed in the next chapter. Another program he considered outstanding was at the South Florida State Hospital in Hollywood, Florida. This center was started about nine years ago, and it, like Western State, relies heavily on the self-help group Synanon model.[3] The Intensive Treatment Program for Sexual Aggressives at Minnesota Security Hospital also impressed Brecher: "[It] has considerably more emphasis on sex education, which I very much approve of. It is still too new and much too much in a state of change and development to evaluate. I have high hopes that in a few years it will be comparable to the other two outstanding programs in Florida and Washington.

"On the out-patient community side," Brecher said, "the program in the Juvenile Protection Parole Department in San Jose, California, is a very effective one. It's in the juvenile department for a very interesting reason. Prior to 1972, whenever an incest case was reported, the long arm of the law clasped its hand on the father's shoulder, ripped him out of the household into a maximum security institution, with a sentence of one to fifty years. Simultaneously, the juvenile protection people took the offended-against child and yanked him or her out of the family and the child was put into a shelter and eventually into a foster home. This left the wife and children on welfare, and the family absolutely destroyed.

"Early in this process, a lawyer usually appeared on the

scene and left with a retainer of between $3,000 and $10,000 to defend the offender against the criminal procedure, so that even if the rest of the process didn't bankrupt the family, this was sure to do it. The juvenile probation workers dealt with the children. About four years ago they rebelled, and said that they were not going to stay in this business of destroying families. There must be a better way. For this reason the program grew up in the Juvenile Probation Parole Department, and it remains there. A first-rate clinical psychologist, who calls himself a humanistic psychologist, was brought in and today the system is very different.

"Immediately following arrest, the father goes to an open institution, where he serves only nights and weekends. He keeps his job so that he remains the provider for the family, even though he is no longer living with them. Within hours after his arrest, he receives a phone call from a member of a self-help group called Parents United. The man says, 'Look, I hear you've got a problem, and I had the same one three years ago. Do you want to come and rap?' Every offender wants to. One plus value is that he doesn't have to pay the attorney's fee. At the same time a woman from the same group who had a similar problem is calling his wife to offer her assistance. The wife's treatment begins at that point.

"This organization is now composed of a group of seventy-five or eighty couples. It also includes a significant number of men whose wives have split from them. People stay in this volunteer self-help program often for two or three years because they find it so useful. Curiously enough, there are a number of volunteer familes who have not fallen afoul of the law, but who have learned about the program. They say, 'Look, do we have to be arrested, or can we come in and join you?' and I find this exciting. It is, to date, primarily for incest families. They are beginning to take some child-molestation families, where the molested child is not in the family, but in the neighborhood, or somewhere else. I see no reason why this cannot be generalized to some other forms of sex offenses," Brecher declared.

One group working to encourage this kind of self-help program is Prisoners Against Rape (P.A.R.) which was founded by William Fuller and Larry Cannon in 1973. It is composed of men who have committed rape and women who are active in antirape groups and task forces of feminist organizations. Individuals interested in combating rape, and other incarcerated persons, are also included. They believe that by forming an organization that brings together persons affected by or affecting rape, they are better able to understand the causes as well as the preventive measures that must be taken before this crime can be eliminated.

At present, most of the P.A.R. prisoners are at the Lorton Complex at Lorton Prison in Lorton, Virginia. The first year of P.A.R.'s existence was devoted to consciousness raising among the imprisoned members. They dealt with the motivations for raping, attitudes toward women and sex, myths about rape, and general education about the subject. From these sessions came the basic ideas for a prison-based antirape program. Since the organization was started by the prisoners without help from the prison administration, it is different from any other program involving rapists. Its aim is not simply the reeducation of offenders, but the reeducation of society with the goal of combating rape. They hope that in the future many prisons will have P.A.R. chapters and that more rape crises centers, task forces, and individuals will become members.

The P.A.R. program consists of lectures from the perspective of former rapists and other knowledgeable people, including women who have been raped. They study the legal, social, mythical, and medical aspects of rape, and its causes and prevention. They form discussion groups to allow the many persons dealing with, or affected by, rape to communicate with one another. In this way they better understand the subject and each other. These groups bring together former rapists, victims, researchers, doctors, policemen, corrections officials, feminists, judges, and lawyers. They write up their findings for distribution.

Brecher concluded from his program survey that all of the treatment centers have some merit, and they should be continued. Though he wished that many would be much better, he believes that doing anything is better than nothing. None are doing any harm, in his judgment. The only way that we will learn about the sex offender and how to develop good treatment is by trying and studying. Within the next few years, models that are now being tried out are going to prove or disprove themselves and offer much greater guidance to others that are getting started. From one point of view, all of them are experimental. This is where we are now, he observed.

**4**

# How Treatment Centers Differ

In 1977 I visited thirteen of the less than thirty sex-offender treatment centers in the United States. I talked with the offenders, the counselors, and the administrators of the programs in an effort to find out firsthand what therapies were offered and their relative effectiveness. Seven of these programs are in maximum security settings; one, in a moderate security setting; the last five operations treat sex offenders as outpatients. The following descriptions of eleven of these programs illustrate the range of facilities available.

## The Treatment Program for Sexual Offenders at Western State Hospital, Fort Steilacoom, Washington

One of the oldest and best-established centers is at Western State Hospital in Fort Steilacoom, Washington, a sleepy little town sixty miles from Seattle. The hospital itself is not a maximum security installation; the sex-offender unit is in a special locked section and has a maximum capacity of 260 inmates.

This facility is a typical old psychiatric institution: a three-story building containing wards, dayrooms, kitchens, etc.—not brightly decorated, but kept neat and clean. The doors to each unit are paneled glass. One offender in each unit is held responsible for the key to the front door.

The following general description and evaluation of the program are largely based on a report made by Richard Seely, director of the Intensive Treatment for Sexual Aggressives Program at the Minnesota Security Hospital. This report was written after Seely returned from a two-week study visit in 1974. It provides information and evidence that even under an archaic system an effective and extraordinarily economical treatment program can be developed.

The Western State program is responsible for the majority of Washington's committed sexual offenders. It is looked upon as the center for consultation, training, and research in this field by courts, institutions, and agencies throughout the state. Its purpose is to provide an effective and economical evaluation and treatment service for habitual sex offenders. These are individuals who are of special concern to the public and who otherwise would simply be imprisoned with little likelihood of corrective treatment. Although standard psychiatric and psychological examination procedures are also routinely employed, the center has developed a unique guided self-help approach. It represents a major departure from traditional psychiatric and correctional methods.[1]

Dr. George McDonald, the late director of the program, has written about its therapy: "From the onset, the sexual psychopath is made to feel that although his deviant behavior is deplored, he is heartily welcomed by a group who understands him and will help him to change if he wishes to do so." Although the offender views himself as a loathsome person who would be despised if his behavior were known, he is accepted by the program participants as a fellow human being in need of help. McDonald further wrote: "Deviant sexual behavior is learned behavior, and therefore subject to modification if methods can be developed to break up old habit patterns. Sex offenders, following the example set by Alcoholics Anonymous and other groups, can do a great deal to help each other overcome their deviant behavior if given the right kind of direction and guidance by staff. The process for learning or re-learning acceptable behavior must relate as much as possible to the realities of living in society at large."[2]

In his report Seely pointed out the effects of the program. "A versatile, small, specially trained staff, along with citizen volunteers, are used directly in the treatment process. In this way, the center is able to provide a specialized service at a lower per diem cost than the adult correctional system. Also there is a shorter length of institutional residence. They have achieved approximately a five-times lower recidivism rate for offenders discharged from treatment compared to men placed on parole from adult correctional systems. During fiscal 1972, the center provided evaluations on one hundred and twenty offenders. It treated one hundred and twenty-two inpatient men and gave follow-up services to twenty-seven offenders. Twenty-six offenders' wives received weekly marital counseling. In terms of custody, the program was successfully conducted within an open mental hospital environment. Traditional restraints are not used. They experienced no higher escape rate than for adult correctional systems which was approximately three percent during the past two years."

The extraordinarily low cost and relative effectiveness of the program are made possible by centering its structure and procedures around small, largely self-administering treatment groups. Each of these groups of approximately fifteen offenders is under the close daily guidance of a specially trained therapy supervisor. Carefully selected patient leaders are responsible for every aspect of the offenders' daily living, that is, his custody and supervision, psychotherapy, work assignments, recreation, and family relationships.

The new offender admitted for observation is immediately assigned at random to one of these groups. He is oriented on basic hospital and program rules, and directed to begin writing his autobiography. This is the first tool of the psychotherapy process. If retained for treatment, following three months of close observation, he remains with the same group throughout his entire treatment of at least three years. He experiences fifteen months of full inpatient residence, three months of work-release and eighteen months of follow-up treatment. In order to earn a "safe to be at large" recommendation and commence his work-release and outpatient phases of treatment, he must accomplish four basic treatment objectives: (1) recognize his deviant behavior patterns; (2) understand their origin and operation; (3) make a firm commitment to a responsible code of behavior; and (4) demonstrate through daily behavior on the hospital grounds that he is ready for community living.

The program maintains that its first responsibility is the protection of society. This goal is achieved by developing within the offender a new sense of pride in being able to recognize and control his deviant impulses. He must be able to govern his relationships with other human beings by concern for their feelings and rights. The program is based on the premise that this growth can be achieved only in an environment providing opportunities and choices similar to community living.

The program techniques have been developed exclusively through intensive work with sex offenders at Western State Hospital over the past fourteen years. However, it is felt that the self-help concept structure and techniques probably are transferable to other settings and other types of offenders. It is quite possible, therefore, that this program has developed an effective and economically feasible alternative to the prison system.[3]

I lived at Western State Hospital for four days and nights, sleeping at the nurses' residence, which is about five blocks from the therapy center. I walked the distance every morning, passing patients wandering over the grass, laughing, crying, muttering monologues, staring into space. At night I was picked up from the center by a patrol car and delivered to my room. One evening, as I enthused to the patrolman over the excellence of the treatment program, he said: "I don't like the way they run it. The security is too loose. No wonder so many run off." The truth, I informed him, is that no more escape from there than from prison.

My day at Western State began at 9:30, and ended at about midnight or whenever the last therapy session was over. The first morning, I was asked to attend a policy meeting composed of two leaders from each of the thirteen sex-offender groups, plus their therapy supervisors (one for each group). Problems and other business were presented by the leaders and discussed by the members as a whole.

At the end of the meeting, two young men were introduced to me as my hosts during my stay. One was a very young man (I guessed about nineteen) with sparkling brown eyes, black wavy hair, and a flashing, friendly smile. The second man appeared a little older, had red curly hair that hung to his shoulders and a copious beard. He greeted me warmly, introduced himself and his companion, and briefly described the program schedule. Because of his easy manner and articulate speech, I addressed him as a therapist. He laughed and said, "Oh, no, I'm a resident."

My hosts invited me to join their group (called East Group) for meals as well as therapy. Each day we lined up for the food at the hospital cafeteria, and ate together at one table. No therapists were present and I was the only visitor. Meal time was limited to thirty minutes, offering me the choice of eating or talking. I found conversing more important, so most of my servings ended up in the garbage.

Before the first session, the therapy supervisor for East Group had given me some statistics about the men whose lives I was about to share. Incest, child molestation, and rape were the most common offenses, and some were guilty of all three. The men were predominantly from lower middle-class families, a third of them were married, 27 percent were divorced, and half had children. Two-thirds began their deviant behavior as teenagers, or younger. Most of them had passed or would pass the first ninety-day observation period—of those remaining, one-third would fail to finish the program. These averages were based on the center's fourteen years of operation.

The first therapy session was scheduled that afternoon from 2:30 to 4:30, and we met every day at the same time. The evening sessions began at 7:30 and ended around midnight. Maximum group membership is twenty; there were seventeen men in our group. We sat in a circle, and at the initial meeting we all introduced ourselves. The format used was: "I'm John Jones, am twenty-five years old, and have been here fourteen weeks. My outlet [offense] is rape and incest. Welcome." Their physical appearances ranged from large to small, and from homely to handsome. Nineteen to forty-three was the age span. With the exception of one black and one Mexican, all the men were Caucasian. All but one were heterosexual. They lived in the state of Washington; their length of time in the program varied from one day to outpatient status. Since it is a self-help therapeutic community, the therapy supervisor joined us only occasionally.

The first few months of treatment are the most arduous for the offender—he hides his guilt behind a self-protective shield. Cracking this façade is a painful but necessary first step. I fortunately had the opportunity to watch this process the second day of my therapy observation, when a tall, slender man said he wanted to speak to the group. The room grew silent and the men give him their full attention. "I won't see my girl for three months," he declared. "She says she's going on a trip, but I know it's all over for us. She'll never come back! I don't know how I'll live without her!" His chin trembled and tears spilled down his cheeks. Encouraging voices came from the group. "Don't hold back!" "Let it all hang out!" "Don't be afraid to cry!" "It's all right!" His static words broke through the sobs. "I've hurt so many women. I hurt so much myself. I'm no fuckin' good! I want to die!"

Two men put their arms around his heaving shoulders while others urged him to continue talking. When the man completely lost control, the group leader got up from his chair, walked over, and embraced him warmly. One by one the other men repeated his gesture of affection and understanding. I felt such compassion that I involuntarily rose up ready to join the group; however, remembering my visitor status just in time, I sank back into my seat. I knew that another member was ready for the next step on the long road to recovery.

After the last session of the fourth evening, I thanked the men for including me in their group and said that I felt more than casually acquainted with each one of them. To my surprise and delight, they responded by presenting me with a "Certificate of Innovation." It reads: "This is to certify that Bart Delin successfully completed the first phase of her development and is entitled to all earned rights, privileges, and one equal share in the Philosophy of East Group, Unit of Behavior Innovation." The document is given to all the men as they complete their first step. As they rose to shake my hand, I knew that a new dimension had been added to my life.

## Patuxent Institute, Jessup, Maryland

In 1951 the state of Maryland enacted a statute creating Patuxent Institute as a maximum security treatment center. It stated in part that only offenders judged to be "defective delinquents" were eligible, and defined such persons as "individuals who, by the demonstration, of persistent aggravated, anti-social or criminal behavior, evidence a propensity to criminal activity."

Before a person could be sent to Patuxent, he had to have been sentenced for the crime of which he was convicted, and the term of imprisonment had to be indeterminate. The decision to send him there was made by the sentencing court. The person was then examined by the institute's staff, which consisted of at least one psychiatrist, one psychologist, and one medical physician.

Confinement and treatment were to be terminated only when the institute found the "defective delinquent" reasonably safe to enter society. His release from Patuxent came in one of two ways: (1) he could be granted parole or work release by the Institutional Board of Review or (2) at his own request, he could be released by the court as a result of a hearing.

Since July 1, 1977, the statute governing Patuxent has been changed. The phrase "defective delinquent" has been replaced by "eligible person" and is defined as a person who: (1) has been convicted of a crime and is serving a sentence of imprisonment with at least three years remaining on it; (2) has an intellectual deficiency or emotional unbalance; (3) is likely to respond favorably to the programs and services provided at Patuxent Institute; and (4) can be better rehabilitated through those programs and services than by other incarceration. Fixed sentencing has replaced indeterminate. This last change is the most disturbing to the staff, since they have now lost the right to determine when the men are ready to leave. The possibility of their imposing overlong sentences has been the criticism most often leveled at the institute, and is the prime reason for changing the statute. Eligibility for Patuxent is not based on whether or not the institute believes the inmates are susceptible to therapy. Their concept is that all dangerous criminals should be given a treatment opportunity. If treatment proved to be ineffective, the men could remain all of their lives. Under the present determinate sentencing, they can be released, having received little or no help.

In speaking to staff members, I learned that they feel the new law removes treatment incentive; since treatment is voluntary, the inmates will be tempted to "sit out" their time because it is less demanding. On the other hand, it seems to me that people who volunteer for therapy are more likely to modify their behavior.

The capacity of the institute is 520 men with the ages ranging from sixteen to sixty-five. Of that group, approximately 13 percent are sex offenders. Until this year, when a special sex-offender unit was set up, all types of felons were treated together. The sex offenders I spoke with were enthusiastic about the new group, which they felt was more empathetic.

Surely Patuxent's physical facilities surpass those of the usual more antiquated prison. Instead of rooms stacked to the ceiling, there is one row of cells on each floor. The building is divided into four living sections called tiers. Upon first entering, the prisoner joins Tier One. When the staff determines that an inmate has made progress in rehabilitation, he is moved to the next tier. With each promotion, privileges and freedom of movement are gained, leading to minimum security (another area on the grounds), work release, and then parole. Vocational training is heavily emphasized. Learning a skill and attaining good work habits is considered therapeutic. This theory is in contrast to Western State Hospital's program, which includes no vocational training and encourages these kinds of skills to be learned on the outside.

I had mixed feelings about Patuxent; I sensed an inflexibility in its organization. For instance, they have only one female therapist. She is a social worker who is employed as a mother symbol in the sex-offender unit. The men are encouraged to vent their pent-up anger on her. When I suggested it might be wise to have other women present to create a more normal atmosphere, they said the female guards, of which they had a few, sufficed.

In attempting to evaluate Patuxent's effectiveness, it is important to keep in mind the large number of participants, their wide age span and the seriousness of their crimes. Most treatment programs would consider many of the Patuxent inmates untreatable. Patuxent believes that the once "well-established fact" that chronic offenders do not respond to psychotherapy is rapidly becoming a myth. With sufficient time and modification of therapeutic techniques, offenders will respond positively, they believe. Although there are several therapeutic methods, the single most important factor until now has been time. Whether or not the administration at Patuxent can adjust to the new rules remains to be seen.

## The Adult Diagnostic and Treatment Center, Avenel, New Jersey (formerly the Rahway Treatment Unit, Rahway State Prison)

This center, originally located within Rahway Prison, is now housed in the only freestanding building in the country constructed exclusively for the treatment of sex offenders. Built in 1977, it resembles a contemporary prison; for instance, instead of the usual parallel bars there are bars constructed in geometric designs. In every executive office and meeting room there sits a closed-circuit television set which monitors every activity in the prison. This practice, useful though it may be, gave me the feeling that "big brother" watched over all.

Dr. Ira Mintz, a clinical psychologist, is the superintendent, but William Prendergast, the original director, is the name most closely associated with the institution, for it is he who introduced the ROAR (Re-education of Attitudes

and Repressed Emotions) method of therapy for which the
institute is best known. Prendergast noted that in a large
proportion of cases, sex offenders themselves had been
victims of sexual abuse as children and that many had
blotted out the experiences. He believes that the truth must
surface before effective treatment can occur. During ROAR
treatment, the offender is encouraged to "regress" into
childhood. There he dredges up the trauma of family
abuses.

All therapy, most of which involves self-help groups, is
recorded on video tape so that both the administration and
the inmates can review what takes place. The video tape is
necessary in ROAR therapy, the therapists believe, so that
the offender, who during treatment has gone into what
appears to be a trance, can verify his response. All other
types of therapy are taped for review as well.

I saw one of the ROAR tapes along with the offender who
experienced it. In the video tape the young man went into
an exhausting rage, sweating, screaming, crying, and pound-
ing on a pillow that represented his mother. The other men
in his group surrounded him to keep him from hurting
himself. He told me that it took two days to recover from
the experience, and that it was a week before he had the
courage to look at the tape. For him, ROAR had a healing
effect.

While ROAR is practiced at the program, it is often criticized as being more dramatic than therapeutic, and is
therefore not used as frequently now as it was initially. For
instance, Prendergast claims that in the unconscious state,
hands that were intentionally burned in childhood can again
appear red and raw and that old wounds can open up and
bleed. Such contentions are questioned by many.

There are approximately two hundred inmates at the
center. Eligible offenders are multiple felons who act
compulsively. All sentencing is indeterminate and participation in therapy is optional; about 5 percent refuse therapy,

and some of this group have remained at the center as long as fourteen years. The rest of the residents respond in varying degrees. The center is also slanted toward vocational training; among other skills, the men learn to operate all the video equipment.

I believe this center to be superior to prison, but treatment time is too limited. Therapy groups meet for only one and a half hours once a week. More money should have been invested in comprehensive therapy and less in the grand structure.

## The CASH and Eager Village Programs, Baltimore, Maryland

As I was escorted through the Baltimore jail, the crowding together of human flesh was oppressive and even frightening. One section appeared to be filled with women, attractively dressed and carefully coifed. Some were affectionate and called me "Honey." When I questioned my attendant, he said they were transvestites brought in on charges of prostitution.

Everywhere the men lay on their cots in tiny cells, or peered from behind the bars. An occasional prisoner pushed a dust mop across the hall floor to relieve the monotony. I was told that he got two packs of cigarettes for his trouble.

Rehabilitation in a jail setting is unique to Baltimore, Maryland. The jail itself houses two thousand men; 90 percent are black. (The percentage of urban blacks is 60.) CASH, which stands for Confined Addicts Seeking Help, was created in 1976. It is a therapeutic community within the jail. The thirty drug addicts involved in the program refurbished a section of the jail in preparation for their own treatment center. People from the community furnished the material, and the inmates run the program under the supervision of professional therapists. As a result, fewer guards are needed in that area, thereby cutting the cost of operation. All of these men eat, sleep, and rap together in a closed ward. Their length of stay ranges from three months to three years. This experimental group proved so successful that they now have refurbished an entire floor, which houses three hundred. The second group, called Eager Village, is not restricted to drug addicts, but offers a therapeutic setting for men with a variety of social problems and psychological needs.

The instigator behind CASH is Joseph DeSantis, who is the chief psychologist; however, my contact was Martin Katzenstein, director of treatment services, who is receiving a grant to develop a sex-offender treatment program patterned after these two groups. He said that about 10 percent of the offenders in the Baltimore jail have committed sex crimes, and that separation is important because of the belligerent attitudes the other prisoners have toward them.

I sat in on a CASH rap session. The men were discussing such diverse subjects as the importance of knowing their legal rights and how they feel as members of CASH versus living in the other part of the jail. The man in charge of the group was a resident who had been jailed for two years.

"You've got to accept change," one inmate said. "That's what it's all about up here. Change! 'Cause what you done in the past wasn't right. The things you thought, that you believed in, didn't work or you wouldn't be here." "Let's face it," said another. "When people leave our jails, most of them go back to the same old shit—dope, booze, crime. Our jails ain't the kind of places for positive changes. They're where hardass guys get even harder—and the first offender—he's in for a lot of crap that don't have nothing to do with rehabilitation. All the shit they do on the street, they do in jails. You know they stick people up here. They've got prostitutes, they've got dope dealers. They've got dealers who sell alcohol, and gambling spots. It's just like on the street. To survive, he'll have to be hard. There's no time for thought. Even if he wants to change, he ain't got a chance."

The CASH pamphlet reads: "Your concept is wrong. You're in jail! You're right here. That's reality."

The CASH program cannot develop long-term rehabilitation in most cases. But since jail sentences usually are short-term, at least it does afford the men an opportunity for living in clean surroundings (many of them for the first time in or out of jail), taking pride in where they live and how they look, and for reflecting on past behavior. It also helps them develop a sense of community. Participation is voluntary, and there is a long waiting list. Katzenstein hopes to gradually clean up most of the jail so that everyone who wishes to can be a part of a therapeutic community.

## Intensive Treatment Programs for Sexual Aggressives (ITPSA), Minnesota Security Hospital, St. Peter, Minnesota

Minnesota Security Hospital has all the external appearance of its "snake pit" counterparts—its antiquated, gray structure, its barred windows, make it resemble a prison. The hospital is located in St. Peter, a small, attractive town, seventy miles from Minneapolis.

In 1974 the BEAD (Behavioral Emotional Attitudinal Development) program was instituted at the Minnesota Security Hospital.* It was a forerunner to the hospital's present sex-offender unit and was the first of its kind in Minnesota—e.g., a program in a secure setting set up exclusively for sex offenders—so the methods used were experimental. Financial support came from the Minnesota Department of Public Welfare and a private foundation. It was for a two-year period, to initiate special treatment for sex offenders in Minnesota.

The BEAD program served two main purposes: to demonstrate that sex offenders can be treated and to provide staff

*A complete description of BEAD appears in Appendix C.

with experience in running such a program. Much was learned about what did and did not work, and practices were revised for the present program. Educating the staff was perhaps the most beneficial aspect of BEAD.

Richard Seely, the director of ITPSA, discussed the present program with me. He explained that the purpose of it is to provide an effective and economical assessment and treatment service for sexual offenders in the state of Minnesota. "I believe it is atrocious that we lock sex offenders up for a number of years, turn them loose without any help, and are surprised when they commit the same crime," he said.

Until 1975, Seely told me, everyone was sent either to the hospital or to the Minnesota State Prison for a presentencing examination. If a prisoner came to the hospital, those in charge would advise the judge whether or not they could treat him. Usually they kept those kinds of people who fitted in with their population, those who were mentally ill, who had some kind of psychiatric disturbance. In most cases, the hospital did the presentencing examination. They had the power to recommend to the court which people would return for treatment. At that time the patients were considered mentally ill, and the medical-model application of drugs and one-to-one psychotherapy were used. There was no specific sex-offender treatment program.

"Now those who are referred directly from the courts must report back to the judge within sixty days. The judge can then continue the offender up to two years for treatment. If at the end of that time the hospital staff thinks he needs continued treatment, they go back to the judge. The offender could be released, but in most cases the judge follows the staff's recommendations. If it is felt that the patient is ready to go after two years, he will most likely be released.

"The sex-offender treatment program started because of a need and not because of a crisis. At the hospital sex offenders are treated like any other human beings in trouble, whether mentally retarded, chemically dependent, or mentally ill. Our aim is to help them solve their difficulties so that they can some day be contributing members of society. Many of them were before they came in."

The program believes that the sexual offender can be effectively treated. The treatment process involves a comprehensive program based on therapeutic community, educational, reality, and rational emotive concepts, combined with the techniques used by Masters and Johnson.

It is based on six basic philosophical points:

1. Human behavior is learned; therefore, both responsible and irresponsible sexual behavior is learned behavior.

2. The sexual offender has used other people as mere objects for his own gratification; he must learn to respect the rights and feelings of other people.

3. Responsibility in the therapeutic community, increased sensitivity to others and self through interaction in small- and large-group therapy, and understanding human sexual behavior are the goals; learning is best when the learners are expected to carry the major responsibility; the role of the staff is to organize, guide, and teach.

4. All problems must be dealt with within the context of reality and all aspects of the treatment process reflect the demands of responsible behavior in our society; the learner must recognize reasonable behavioral alternatives and choose to behave in an ethical, responsible manner.

5. Sustained appropriate behavior, understanding of self, and ability to deal effectively with problems are the criteria.

6. Learning and treatment continue as long as necessary while the learner is applying his new behaviors and values under community conditions.[4]

Currently, the program serves thirty-seven male residents, ranging in age from seventeen to forty. Offenses include rape, incest, and child molestation. The average predicted stay for new admissions is approximately thirty-six to forty-eight months.

The residents are housed in a thirty-two-bed unit of

Minnesota Security Hospital. The unit operates according to therapeutic community principles, which include mutual twenty-four-hour monitoring of each other's behavior and collective responsibility for the total operation of the unit.

Present staff consists of one unit director, two full-time psychologists, one half-time psychologist, two social workers, one special teacher, one clerk-steno, two recreation therapists, and one attendant guard-counselor. All staff are members of the treatment team and meet daily to discuss the treatment process, unit problems, group therapy, and resident progress, Seely explained.

The staff and everyone connected with the program are required to take a sex education course. "In the beginning I taught it on a low-key level as a division of a life-adjustment series," Seely said. "It was more like a physical plumbing course. Later, we dealt with how people felt about their own sexuality. Soon nearly everyone involved began seeing sex offenders as human beings. They cared about what the men had gone through that had brought them into this institution."

The treatment process consists of group therapy, a specialized therapeutic community, crisis intervention, family therapy, and group social and recreational activities. Community meetings, held approximately five hours per week, are attended by all unit members and are led by the unit director. The focus is on learning effective communication skills and understanding interpersonal relationships, dealing with personal feelings and inappropriate behavior, and defining the treatment process. Group therapy, held ten to twenty hours per week, and married-couples therapy, held two and one-half hours per week, are supervised by male-female cotherapist teams and focus on individual histories, behavior, attitudes, responsibilities, and problem solving.

The confrontation inherent in group therapy forces self-analysis and encourages the resident to deal with his past aggressive behavior, his present lack of consideration for the rights of others and other predatory and manipulative tendencies.

Each resident progresses through six phases and fifteen steps of progress in the treatment process, ranging from total programming within Minnesota Security Hospital to an outpatient therapy relationship. Seely talked about the results to date: "Evaluation of residents involved in the program for one year or more seems to indicate significant improvement in behavior, communication skills, concern for others, and awareness of self. These perceptions are based on day-to-day monitoring of behavior, psychological test results, psychiatric evaluation, peer evaluation, group involvement, and overall attitude and approach to problems. All residents are expected to become completely involved in the treatment process. Any elopement, contraband, physical assaultiveness, or sexual misconduct constitutes a violation of the resident's contract and will usually result in immediate transfer off the unit."

Seely admitted that the program is basically modeled after the treatment program at Western State Hospital in Washington, which reports an 8.9 percent recidivist rate (91.1 percent success rate). He believes this program has the opportunity to demonstrate equal success in Minnesota.

## Alpha House, Minneapolis, Minnesota

Alpha House is a community-based treatment center to which multiple felons are referred by the courts and prisons. There are approximately thirty men living there, and sex offenders are treated with the other felons. They consider themselves to be brothers living in a family.

"The house has functioned for only three years, and so far we have a good record," I was told by one resident offender. "The average stay is sixteen to seventeen months. We can't use drugs, not even aspirin. As you can see the building is old, but the family takes good care of it. At first the people in the neighborhood were scared of us, but since we've had some open houses, they think we're okay.

"Alpha House is not a halfway house," he explained. "A halfway house is exactly what the name says—you're half in and half out. You work outside half the time, and you sleep at the house. I don't think a person would have the time to get into himself and deal with behaviors the way we do here. It would be hard to be out in the community, exposed to a lot of negative behavior, and then to come back into a positive environment every night. It wouldn't work with me very good!

"I didn't really want to come here," he confessed. "I wanted to be free, but I didn't have that choice. I thought this was a halfway house and that it would be easy going. I said to myself, 'Well, like, you know, it's not going to be that hard. I'll stay for a couple or three months and then I'll be out.' Well, when the time was up I didn't want to leave because I had learned a lot of things about myself, but not enough to live successfully on the outside. I knew I'd end up in prison again if I left too soon."

He explained the treatment process at Alpha House. "When we first get here we're interviewed to find out if we're motivated enough to go through the program. If we're accepted, we come into the family. For the first thirty days we don't leave the house for anything. We're involved in complete therapy dealing with our behavior. We can't even go out in family functions. After that, we start to work our way into doing things with the family. We learn more acceptable ways to behave. We're completely dependent on each other because it's evident that being on our own didn't work so good. As a new resident becomes more responsible, he is given more freedom. This is done by the vote of his peers and counselors."

Locks on the doors are the only security measures at Alpha House; I was told that there are very few attempts to escape. "The most important thing that we look for in a guy is motivation. I guess we don't think about the possibility of running out the door," said an offender.

"Getting out of prison after doing two or three years is really a heavy blow," said another offender. "There's a lot of fantasizing that goes on about the outside world. But when you get out, you find that society just ain't that great.

"At Alpha House, we learn alternative ways of handling situations—such as not infringing on other people, not being irresponsible, and relating to other people better. Before I came here, making friends was almost impossible because I was pissed off with myself and everyone else. I have learned to feel good about talking to people. My life is becoming worth living instead of no good. I'm thirty years old and this is a new experience for me. I know I'll make it!"

The encounter-group-therapy concept as well as one-to-one counseling are used at Alpha House. There is one resident psychologist and several group leaders. The residents themselves run the groups under the supervision of leaders, many of whom formerly received therapy themselves. Individual counseling is with the psychologist.

I sat in on one of the encounter groups at Alpha. All ten men focused their attention on one fellow member who had displayed irresponsible behavior. He had been using some valuable building equipment in the back yard of the house when a telephone call had made him leave. Instead of first securing the tools, he had left them unattended, making theft possible.

They all "grouped" on him in an effort to get an admission of guilt and a promise for more responsible behavior in the future. At first the man in question attempted to support his behavior by giving excuses—"I intended to come right back—the telephone call was important and I didn't want to waste time." The criticism was harsh and pressing, and eventually the target man gave the desired response.

When inappropriate behavior is repeated, a sign sometimes is hung on the neck of the offender. One resident wore a sign that read, "I act like a baby," and he also was required to wear an external diaper. Some therapists believe that this kind of punishment is too severe and humiliating and therefore destructive. Alpha House obviously disagrees.

Of the total population of Alpha House, about eight are sex offenders. (Of course the number varies.) That they are treated with all the other felons I consider a weakness; however, the sex offenders I interviewed found the therapy of value to them.

## The Center for Rape Concern, Philadelphia, Pennsylvania

This outpatient program is the oldest of its kind in the country. It began in 1955 under the direction of the late Dr. Joseph Peters, a psychoanalyst, when he persuaded other psychiatrists in the area to devote one night a week to treating sex offenders without pay.

Getting the courts to refer sex offenders on probation proved to be more difficult, however. For decades one of the prime provisions of probation in Pennsylvania and many other states was that released offenders must not associate with other offenders. This stipulation, of course, would eliminate the possibility of group therapy. It was difficult to convince judges that a change was desirable. They were especially concerned that offenders on drugs would precipitate the distribution of narcotics. Psychoanalysts were not highly respected by the courts either.

These objections ultimately were overcome by periodic meetings with court administrators; close cooperation was absolutely necessary. Finally a procedure was agreed upon. Selected sex offenders who were judged amenable to help were required during probation to attend at least sixteen weekly group therapy sessions. Their probation officers were the liaisons and also recorded the attendance. What really was provided was a service that previously was available only to offenders able to pay.

The program was initiated at the Philadelphia General Hospital, and over the first ten years, sixteen hundred sex offenders took part. At first they separated the various types of offenders (e.g., child molesters, voyeurs, exhibitionists, rapists, etc.). This procedure is no longer used.

After ten years, Dr. Peters and his associates made a follow-up study of ninety-two alumni of the treatment program. They compared what had happened to them with a similar group of sex offenders who had been on probation without therapy. The original offenses of the therapy group were more serious than those of the untreated group. Despite this difference, the treated group fared much better than those untreated. Twenty-seven percent of the untreated group were rearrested during the two-year follow-up period, compared with only 3 percent of the treated group. They were also rated on sexual adjustment, and again those treated rated much higher.

There were shortcomings to the study, however. The follow-up period (two years) was too short and the use of comparison groups rather than controlled groups (starting with a common pool of offenders and then assigning them by lot to one group or the other) made the findings less reliable.[5]

In 1966, significant changes were made in the program. Instead of the participation of random probation officers, six were chosen to become specialists in handling sex offenders. Forty weekly group meetings were required instead of sixteen. In 1970, their services were expanded to include victims—not, of course, in the same group. One thousand and thirty-nine victims were brought to the hospital in 1973, and the next year there was an increase of forty-three. Half were adults, eighteen years and older; one third were adolescent, age thirteen to seventeen; and the rest were children, age twelve or younger. A follow-up home-visit program was established where a social worker was assigned to visit each victim in her home within forty-eight hours after her visit to the hospital emergency room. The social worker offered support and a willingness to arrange for further care if needed and desired.

The addition of weekly couples' groups was instigated in 1974, with male and female cotherapists. Thus the program, which began as psychoanalytic, has developed into one that uses the newer sociosexual approach. The Center for Rape Concern also deals with cases of incest where fathers, mothers, and children are treated. This kind of therapy often makes it possible for the families to remain together. With the addition of these latest services, this is the most complete outpatient program of which I have heard. They have now moved from the Philadelphia General Hospital to a downtown business office, where the location is more central and the space more adequate.

## The Center for Behavior Therapy, Minneapolis, Minnesota

This center is a privately operated fee-for-service treatment program where people with such diverse problems as obesity, alcoholism, and sex offenses are treated as outpatients. It belongs to the American Psychological Association and adheres to the criteria established through the State Licensing Act.

The center offers one-to-one treatment with a psychologist, but includes family counseling as well. One of the controversial techniques that it occasionally uses is aversive therapy, which at this particular center involves introducing a mild electric shock at an appropriate time in an effort to discourage an inappropriate behavior pattern. Aversive conditioning is feared by some as an instrument to produce undesired personality changes. In the past, homosexual behavior was coercively changed to heterosexual by this method (not at this center), so homosexuals especially distrust its use.

William Duffy, executive director of the center, described how he uses aversive conditioning. "Some [of the sex offenders] have highly obsessive compulsive behaviors," he said. "They are similar to neurotic anxieties that others who aren't sex offenders show. At the center, we try to help people learn new deportment that is incompatible with the old; we work with the whole person rather than singling out isolated behaviors. For sex offenders who are obsessive and compulsive, we use aversive conditioning."

According to Duffy, aversive conditioning is a technique that really does not work unless it is continually repeated. Temporary suppression of the obsessive behavior is the reason for its usage. The interruption is just long enough for the man to concentrate on learning new behavioral patterns which are incompatible with the past, and are more rewarding to himself and others.

Duffy explained how aversive conditioning is used: "For example, if a man is a child molester, we have him fantasize, and then show first a picture of a child, then another of an adult woman. At a particular point, the offender signals us with 'Stop!' It means that he is fantasizing have sexual relations with the child. Then we give him a small electric shock. The whole purpose is to remove some of the reinforcing components of that mental image which he has usually satisfied by masturbating. We want to refocus his thought pattern for a while, and I emphasize for a while, because the effect of the treatment doesn't last. It's only short-term therapy.

"This change happens only when it becomes difficult to impossible for the man to think about his particular obsession. However, prior to that, aversive conditioning isn't used exclusively. Along with it, we give behavioral, educational, marriage, and financial counseling. Whatever is necessary to help the person be more effective in his daily living is employed."

Aversive conditioning to many people implies *Clockwork Orange* treatment. It is a highly controversial technique. I asked the senior technician at the Center for Behavior Therapy how he administers it.

"First the client relaxes as much as possible, then I take the electrodes from the shocker and place them on the dominant forearm, securing them with rubber bands," he explained. "The power comes from a flashlight battery. We adjust the intensity of the shocker to suit the individual's needs and tolerance. Levels on the shockers are adjustable in milliamperes, which are the units of intensity, from zero to ten. At its highest current strength, the arm will probably raise just a little bit off the chair. We aim to produce just enough pain to avoid the fantasy that they are having.

"Usually we start out shocking the client at about a quarter of a second at five milliamperes. That's where most people find a fairly reasonable tolerance level, but a point at which they can feel the shock."

At my request, the technician attached the equipment to my forearm, and gave me a shock. It felt like intense static electricity. He said that the strength used on me was the same that they apply when the treatment begins. This is two milliamperes under the maximum.

Duffy defends the use of aversive conditioning. "I deplore the false information about aversive conditioning that is spread. Many believe that there is a loss of freedom and dignity. The technology is powerful," he admitted. "We use it in a positive way to help people control themselves. There is often an emotional reaction to the subject, because the treatment is confused with electrical, convulsive therapy where a strong shock is passed through the brain. What we use is mildly painful, produces no tissue damage, and is used as infrequently as possible. People who are adamantly opposed to this kind of therapy should read some of the letters I've received from prisoners. They've said that two or three hundred shocks (and we don't give anywhere near that many) would not be more painful than one day spent in prison.

"After the program gets started, in order to minimize the cost, we let the men shock themselves. When they see some positive benefits, the amount of discomfort experienced apparently is much less than the pain of the fantasy."

Most of the center's referrals come from the courts, prisons, parole officers, and health-care centers. Up to December 1974, they had worked with sixty-eight sex offenders. Of those, four have repeated their offense. Three of those were exposers, and two of the three were mentally retarded.

I asked Duffy how long an offender usually stays in the program. "The length of time spent in treatment varies," he explained. "For individuals who have been in prison, a more intensive program is needed because of the negative reinforcement they have experienced. Others don't need as long an intensive care.

"About 75 percent of the sex offenders that come to the center are married and they stay with their families while undergoing therapy. We work with the wives, children, in-laws, and whoever is going to have a major influence on their lives. The center also treats some of the sex offenders who are living in Alpha House, which is a community-based treatment center.

"Theoretically, you should be able to treat all sex offenders," Mr. Duffy contends, "but that would smack too much of involuntary mind control, which I oppose. Unless people are really willing—and I'm speaking of everybody we treat, no matter what their problems—we refuse to give them any help."

## Outpatient Treatment Clinic for Special Offenders, Baltimore, Maryland

Dr. Jonas Rappaport, a forensic psychiatrist and chief medical officer of the Supreme Bench of Baltimore, heads this clinic, which was established in 1972 to serve sex offenders referred by the courts representing statewide counties; most of the offenders come from the city of Baltimore. Almost all are on probation; their offenses for the most part are voyeurism, exhibitionism, and incest. The program accepts only those offenders who are judged suitable for the treatment. Its goals are to help participants achieve greater awareness of their problems, and to help them attain sufficient control over their impulses to prevent a recurrence of the antisocial behavior.

The sex offenders are referred to the program by the Maryland Department of Corrections after their convictions. Probation officers administer the clinic and serve as cotherapists in the program. The clinic sessions are held once a week from 5:15 P.M. to 6:45 P.M., and attendance is part of the participant's probation requirement. The probationers are charged one to five dollars per session, depending on their ability to pay, but this represents a small portion of the operational cost.

In the fall of 1977, I attended one of the four weekly groups that serve a total of thirty-two men. There were eight men in my group, with one therapist. The format was quite unstructured, with the men discussing whatever came to mind. Two subjects dominated the evening: homosexuality (several told of annoying experiences, such as being stared at and grabbed by their buttocks on the street) and how to control a belligerent temper. The therapist suggested that in each case the base of the problem was insecurity about masculinity. The men were unwilling to admit to this weakness; I agreed with the leader.

It is difficult for me to evaluate accurately the success of this program, having experienced such a small sampling. Nevertheless, it is clear that requiring the participation of probation officers in the group is very helpful. In too many cases probation officers communicate with their probationers on a monthly basis only, and the relationship is a policing one rather than one of friendly concern. By getting involved in the therapy, the officers gain more understanding of the sexual offenders' problems and the offenders are given an opportunity to see their probation officers as people.

The Outpatient Clinic for Special Offenders was patterned somewhat after the Philadelphia plan (the Center for Rape Concern). The sharing of good ideas should be practiced by all the programs, it seems to me.

## The Program in Human Sexuality, University of Minnesota, Minneapolis, Minnesota

This program was conceived as an adjunct to the University Medical School. For the first time a course on human sexuality was offered to medical students. It was soon expanded to include other professionals, such as lawyers, judges, ministers, legislators—professionals who are as deficient in sex education as are average Americans, even though the nature of their jobs requires special knowledge in this area.

The two-day seminars explore sexual behaviors in their many forms by using visual media and discussion groups. They were used as part of the experimental, and now defunct, BEAD Program at the Minnesota Security Hospital.*

Dr. Richard Chilgren, former director of the human sexuality program, explained the positive effects that the seminars had on all of the participants—those in the helping

*See Appendix B.

professions, as well as the sex offenders undergoing BEAD: "I believe this program is a unique form of sexual health-care delivery, different in the sense that it wrestles with these basic problems that people have in relating to each other. Courses include primarily intense seminars which deal with attitudes not usually expressed openly. The professionals get in touch with their own sexual behavior and the behavior of others. In this way, they can separate their feelings from their professional work long enough to openly and honestly deal with these sensitive, touchy subjects.

"Among professionals who deal with sexual problems and who aren't trained in this area (ministers, lawyers, doctors), there is a tendency to look upon whatever they do themselves sexually as being normal. I don't like the word 'normal.' I think 'standard feeling or condition' might be more descriptive. They, like everyone else, have a wide range of sexual behaviors. It's like a fingerprint; everyone is unique. Defining who is normal is risky.

"The common weakness that many have who are attempting to deal with sexual behavior, is a lack of identification," Dr. Chilgren declared. "By separating 'them' from 'us', the professionals really don't have to make an effort to understand the other person. The impression given is: 'I wouldn't do anything like that under any circumstances!'

"We see a great variety of reactions from the groups that experience our two-day seminars. Some are happy because there's something they can identify with; others are angry and frustrated because there's something they don't like. Interestingly enough, the person next to you may be going through the same reaction, but in the opposite order. They can be turned on by something you don't like, and turned off by something you do. After the participants talk it through, they often find they can respect each other's differences."

Chilgren said that he especially enjoyed observing the sex

offenders who experienced the program. "They'd say, 'Wow, this is the first real help I've had with this problem. There's something here that I can identify with.' They realized that the feelings were normal; it was the way in which they handled them that was wrong. They felt less ostracized, while at the same time their antisocial behavior was not condoned. The men were given a chance to look at themselves in another light—one which didn't separate them from the rest of society," he explained.

"Recently the American Academy of Pediatrics observed that children by the age of fifteen have watched fourteen to fifteen thousand acts of violence, either on television or in their neighborhoods. 'How many acts of intimacy have children seen at that age?' someone asked. The estimate is three to five, or none. I despair at its being permissible to see people hurt, but not loved. Handling this situation is difficult for many and it can produce warped ideas about sexual feelings.

"Sex offenders who have been incarcerated represent a sort of end of the spectrum," Chilgren added. "Their behaviors depict the extreme of how we all behave. We've been brought up in a culture that represses our sexual functions and feelings; when we recognize their presence, we often have feelings of guilt. This is perfectly normal, I believe.

"According to a Minnesota statute, a large number of couples, married and unmarried, are sex offenders. The law reads that all oral sex is illegal. Such archaic laws may have a subconscious effect on some people's behavior.

"Historically, one of the purposes of punishment in prisons was to separate people from their own sexual outlets," he continued. "I would see that as more painful than the physical confinement because intimacy and closeness are necessary components to all of us."

Chilgren spoke of new studies that are coming out of the National Institutes of Mental Health: "They suggest that one of the things leading to violence is the deprivation of physical pleasure in our early years; there is laboratory and anthropological evidence to support this position."

## Juvenile Sex Offender Program, Seattle, Washington

Treating juveniles as sex offenders is an innovative idea. Courts and social workers historically have been loath to recognize the seriousness of the sexual aspect of a juvenile crime. For instance, if a boy has stolen a car and molested a little girl as well, he will more likely be charged with the theft only. Too often the attitude is the old "boys will be boys"—it's perfectly normal for boys to "play around" sexually.

The Juvenile Sex Offender Program at the Adolescent Clinic of the University of Washington in Seattle was created in 1976. Referrals are made to the clinic through the courts and directly by the families. At present there is such limited funding that the therapists are restricted to evaluating their clients. However, this is done over a period of twelve to fourteen sessions and, according to program therapist Gary Wenet, that short time is often enough to correct the deviancy. The parents also are included in the therapy. The program has been promised a grant that will make expansion possible.

The most usual juvenile offense is child molestation, which, as we have seen, often starts out as curiosity about sex. It develops into deviant behavior when a boy is older than the victim and the act is coercive. This development usually appears as the offender becomes less sure of his manhood, as well as of his own self-worth.

Discovering this tendency when the offender is young is important as a possible deterrent to more serious crimes. Too many parents ignore their son's behavior as a "normal boyish prank." Whenever sexual relations are forced, they are potentially dangerous, and the cause should be treated.

Seattle's Juvenile Sex Offender Program, as well as the one in San Jose, California (described earlier by Edward Brecher), are steps in the right direction. It is hoped that other states will follow their examples.

# 5

# Evaluating Behavioral Change Through Therapy

Experiencing group sessions with sex offenders convinced me that all therapy is of some value, and many methods are producing impressive results. Positive changes in the offenders' lives benefit society as well.

As the programs I visited show, we are witnessing an accelerated growth of more humane, socially accountable therapies (such as reality therapy) in which people with problems depend on others with similar difficulties for help, as well as getting individual counseling. The influence that human beings have on one another has long been noted, but has not been applied extensively in therapeutic practice. We know, finally, that sex offenders are not mentally ill by clinical definition; therefore they do not need to be "cured" by professionally trained practitioners.

Reality therapy contrasts with the earlier psychoanalytical approach in its emphasis on people's responsibility for their own behavior. Putting the blame on someone else, e.g., one's parents, excuses the necessity for facing the here and now. Explaining and excusing conduct are different. The past cannot be changed—only the present is subject to modification.

At the present time, great emphasis is placed on group psychotherapy, with special concentration on peer pressure. Offenders who have proven to be poor candidates for traditional treatment approaches seem in many cases responsive to this new therapy. Untrained persons have incredible potential for giving help if only they are allowed to use their talents.

According to Dr. William Glasser in his book, *Reality Therapy,* psychiatry must be concerned with two basic psychological needs: the need to love and be loved; the need to feel worthwhile to ourselves and to others. Glasser believes that the severity of the symptom reflects the degree to which the person fails to meet these needs satisfactorily. No matter how bizarre or irrational the behavior appears to others, it always has meaning to the person: a rather ineffective but nevertheless necessary attempt to gratify these fundamental wants.

One way to satisfy these needs is to be involved with other people, Glasser feels. Involvement, of course, means a great deal more than simply associating with others. It must be a shared relationship of care and concern. Most of us experience this affinity with parents, spouses, close friends, or others. When there is no closeness with at least one other human being, we begin to deny the world around us, and to lose the ability to satisfactorily meet our needs. The focus of positive therapy, therefore, is on present behavior, about which something can be done. The patient is forced to face the consequences of his or her behavior. Was it right or wrong? What are the results for the offender? Realistic behavior occurs when a person considers and compares the immediate and future consequences of his or her actions.[1]

It is encouraging to note the progressive changes that are appearing in the treatment of human behavior. Many of the original programs used the medical or psychiatric model where the offenders were seen as patients, considered ill, and were treated only on a one-to-one basis. Now, as we have seen, many other forms of therapy are being tried. Some of these are:

1. Self-help groups modeled after Alcoholics Anonymous
2. Therapeutic communities, modeled after drug treatment programs
3. Family therapy—including group participation of wives with their husbands in an effort to help both spouses better understand themselves and each other
4. The teaching of attitudinal changes in relating to friends—especially to women—and to themselves in particular
5. Eclectic approach—exchanging ideas with other programs in an effort to tailor treatment to the individual offender

All the programs strongly support the concept that *human beings can change* and that environment is the most determining factor in how one develops. The prison atmosphere creates the convict personality which manipulates, "cons," and struggles for power through coercion. This kind of behavior modification is not planned; it is inherent in the incarceration itself.

Dramatic changes in treatment models occurred in the early 1970s. Sex reeducation is one such change. (Many sex offenders lack accurate information about even the simplest sexual responses; their attitudes tend to be puritanical.) Material that before 1950 would have been considered pornographic is often used as a part of treatment in the form of sex education. Attitudes of therapists toward masturbation also have undergone profound change. Many participants feel more guilty about masturbating than they do about raping. Some programs encourage masturbation without guilt feelings or assaultive fantasies. Other programs encourage the clinical use of nakedness to replace shame of body with pride of appearance.

Efforts to personalize the victims of sex offenders instead of objectifying them is also considered an important part of therapy. In some programs victims and offenders exchange audio tapes in which they describe their rape experiences from their different perspectives. One center has an incest victim and an offender working as partners while another has rapists and victims (not their own) rapping together.

Attempts are being made at making the offenders feel more sexually adequate by giving them opportunities to relate to women in therapy sessions. Mixing offenders with nonoffenders in group discussions where the same subjects are examined has proven helpful in mutual understanding.

The use of female cotherapists also helps sex offenders relate to women in general. (Only four treatment programs are headed by women. They are in Hollywood, Florida; Alburquerque, New Mexico; Philadelphia, Pennsylvania; and Buena Vista, Colorado.) As psychologist Asher Pacht, who headed the now defunct Wisconsin Sex Offender Program, commented: "It is incongruous for an individual who may have primary problems in his relationships with mature women to be sentenced to the all-male environment of the typical prison. This is hardly an ideal atmosphere for the development of sociosexual skills necessary for establishing such relationships."

Carole Anne Searle, who works with the Canadian Penitentiary Service, also stressed the need to use women in sex-offender therapy. "In many cases the sexual offender is fearful of women, even hostile towards them, and therefore unable to approach them except in an abusive manner. Also, many view women only as objects for sexual gratification. It is essential that the offender be given opportunity to learn differently—that he can have a normal, friendly relationship with women. This can be done only when he is placed in situations which bring him into daily contact with women

who are willing to work through problems with him and
participate in the role-playing socialization process. He must
learn to talk to and be heard by women, discuss ideas, learn
to laugh with them, argue on occasion, and understand that
they are not threatening or dangerous, thus learning that
there is more to a male-female relationship than sexual confrontation. In essence, they must understand that extensive
interpersonal relationships with women are prerequisite to
normal sexual adjustment in our society. All of these altera-
tions indicate the kind of modifications that are being introduced in sex-offender treatment programs."[2]

Through my visits to treatment centers I learned the signi-
ficance of public education on the subject of sex offenders,
and the necessity for designing and funding many more programs. But the question still remains: how effective are all
these programs, really? Most people believe that the rehabilitation of *any* offender is impossible, and this belief applies
to sex offenders in particular. Usually these opinions come
from those who have little or no knowledge about programs. As we have seen, the professionals I interviewed had
positive feelings about treatment. But what did the offenders themselves feel? During my visits to the various programs I talked with offenders and their families in an effort
to find out how they felt about therapy.

Eddie, a multiple rapist, shared his reactions: "I think
most sex offenders are susceptible to treatment but only if
they want it. It should be an individual choice. It's valuable
to segregate sex offenders in treatment, I think. It's easier
for me to lay out what I've done in a group who have similar problems. I'm not scared they won't accept me after-
wards, because they have done many of the same things. I
feel so relieved when for the first time I can get those things
off my chest.

"The therapists here have a humanistic approach—very
much so. I now feel a lot of respect for myself as a person.
It's true that the people here are in an authoritative position

where they control a vast majority of my life, but I don't have to like that—I'm not expected to. If I have feelings, I'm able to express them and to understand that they are real, but I still have to do what's expected of me."

Eddie told me that he didn't resent the people at the center, and that he was making an effort to humanize his victims and to stop resenting them, too.

"The therapists guide our groups," he said, "but we treat ourselves. It's me who makes the final choice whether or not I reoffend—whether I've become a responsible person or not. It's me that I have to live with the rest of my life."

Sam, another rapist, told me of the experience that led him to therapy. "My raping was caused by a combination of things. For one, I couldn't adjust to civilian life after having been in the army. They have a great system of breaking you down and making you a soldier, but they haven't any way of building you up and making you a civilian again," he remarked. "One day you're in the army, and the next day you're on the streets wondering 'Where am I at?' I began taking drugs and hating everyone. The more hateful I got, the closer I came to committing rape. After having spent five and a half months in a county jail for assault, I was even more bitter. This is when I started raping women. I asked for treatment, but there wasn't any to be had."

After a sixty-day evaluation at a security hospital, Sam went to prison for four months. About then, a treatment program started at a state mental hospital, and he became one of the first participants, remaining there for follow-up therapy. He told me some of what happened to him:

"We underwent a lot of pain through strenuous in-depth group conversations. Sometimes this happened on a one-to-one basis with another guy, and it hurt. I have no qualms about crying in front of other men any more. You know, I've cried so much since I've been here that it's just—you know—I would never have believed I could. Part of my getting well is to hurt and to feel some of the hurt that my victims felt—to really dig deep.

"A group of women from a rape crisis center came to the hospital and met with us. By talking with them we learned how being raped had affected the women's lives. We even cried together. Now I have more empathy for the women I raped. Before that, they weren't real people to me." He ended the interview by saying: "I feel in my guts I will never rape another woman again in my life, but intellectually, I'm not so sure. For the rest of my life I am going to have to say, 'Because I'm a man and because I have the physical power to rape a woman, I have the capability of committing a rape.' Any man that can walk from one place to another, that is physically stronger than a woman, has the potential to be a rapist—and I fall into that category. Not all rapists respond well to therapy, however."

Lenny, a multiple rapist, had been a resident at a community-based halfway house for only one week when I met him. He told me then that he felt much more comfortable in prison, where he had been incarcerated sixteen of his forty years. "Here, I don't know—it's scary. I'm asked all the time about my behavior—what I think about it, where my feelings are at. To get deep down into them things is really scary. I always called people on the outside 'square Johns,' thinking they were the sick ones.

"The men here have done every kind of con job," he told me. "I walked in as a forty-year-old, thinking I'd done more than they had, but no way! Every day I'd get in some argument because they knew where I was coming from and they didn't like it. You can't con anyone here, you've got to be honest. They won't let you get by with any shit."

I visited Lenny again after he had undergone six months of therapy. He seemed to be feeling more secure. "When I first came, I threw out a couple of bones like, 'I raped this girl, molested that girl,' and no one was impressed at all. I got 'grouped on' about once a week, so I'd take a swing at one of the other guys. At first I'd get sore and I still have a short fuse, but I'm learning different ways to deal with people so I won't hurt them or me. It's hard to get rid of the anger," he contended. "I don't think I ever will."

Recently, when Lenny was returning from a work-release program, the urge to rape came over him. Instead of going back to the halfway house, he raped another woman and was sent to prison again. The number of years that Lenny spent in prison as well as his age were probably the prime reasons for his rehabilitation failure.

Robinson Williams, a social worker and cofounder of the Treatment Center for Sexual Offenders at Western State Hospital, states other reasons why some sex offenders cannot accept therapy. "Some are unable to reveal themselves sufficiently; it is not always a deliberate withholding. Sometimes they aren't intelligent enough to put the events of their lives together—especially if they are too old. Others deliberately will not disclose themselves for various reasons. Those people may be so guilt-ridden that they insist on being sent to prison to be punished for what they think is deserved.

"Another group are those who have spent too much time in prison before they got into a treatment operation. The prison code discourages confronting another prisoner. If anyone tries to pry into another's private life, he is likely to have a knife put in his gut. You see, the whole code is different—a totally secretive and hiding culture enforced brutally. Many sex offenders have spent most of their lives in custody—as youngsters in reform schools, as teenagers in reformatories, and then as adults in penitentiaries. Being deceitful, even to close friends, certainly to strangers and all people in authority, becomes a way of life. These people often say, 'Changing the way I've learned to live is just too tough. I'd rather go back to prison where I know the rules.' To change those habits is very, very demanding."

Williams mentioned another characteristic group of sex offenders that is difficult to reach—those who have been raised to believe in the teachings of a fundamentalist religion, where sexuality of any kind is considered dirty. Sex offenders brought up in this way are loners; they put distance between themselves and others. When the pressure to come close to people in the group is really on, these men retreat to the Bible. They suddenly become born-again Christians who want to remain in their rooms reading the Bible and talking to God instead of their fellow men, and it is all done in the name of religion.

"They have been taught that sexuality in and of itself is wrong, rather than the misuse of it. Their families are not loving, do not communicate honestly, and are religious hypocrites. The parents are harsh, judgmental, and distant," Williams explained.

He spoke about the kind of relationship that must develop between the therapist and the offender for therapy to be effective. "Only after offenders are sure that the therapists judge them as fellow human beings instead of monsters will they honestly reveal themselves. Their first response is one of denial. Members of any therapeutic staff must be able to say, 'You have been a very hurtful individual. Until you stop that behavior you cannot have your freedom. We're not going to hurt you in turn for what you've done to other people; helping you to become a better human being is our function. Trust us, show us the bad side of yourself, be willing to deal with it, and then change it.'

"Experiencing the honesty of the other sex offenders in the group helps new men speak truthfully. They are drawn into a confessional experience and begin to face an inner life for the first time. When this feeling catches on, they are relieved because hiding isn't necessary any more. It is a new discovery—one they have never in their lives known before," Mr. Williams declared.

Like most professionals I spoke with, Williams believes that sex offenders will not change from being self-centered and predatory by merely being punished. Punishment only makes them feel more loathsome than before. They really look down on themselves at least as much as does society.

The opinions of offenders and therapists are significant in evaluating the effectiveness of sex-offender therapy, but there is another measurable criterion that many people seek. "It is all well and good to give the offenders more desirable surroundings and a more humane environment," they say, "but does it keep them from repeating crimes?"

According to the *Report on Sex Offenders* by Dr. William Hausman, professor of psychiatry at the University of Minnesota, of 475 sex offenders in Wisconsin treated between 1951 and 1960 and paroled, 9 percent had committed a new sex offense by 1962. In New Jersey, 216 sex offenders were treated and released to the community between June 1967 and August 1974. Six of them were committed for new sex offenses (2.8 percent). In Washington State, 150 sex offenders completed treatment between 1958 and 1968; 9 percent were rearrested, all on less serious charges. At the Ontario Correctional Institute in Brampton, 136 child molesters, most with multiple offenses, have been treated by using a conditioned avoidance paradigm (a sophisticated form of aversive therapy) over the last nine years. In that period of time, 11 have recidivated (8.1 percent).

By comparison, the following are recidivism rates of imprisoned (nontreated) sex offenders. The rates reported range from 18.4 percent to 44 percent. Specifically, 20 percent of Sing Sing prisoners have previous sex offenses (1960). Out of a group of 1551 sex offenders examined in 1965, 18.4 percent of the total group had no previous convictions. But if you consider the men convicted of each crime as a group, the reconviction rates varied from 44 percent for heterosexual aggressions against children to 5.1 percent for heterosexual aggressions against adults.

This brings us to the factors confusing the issue. According to Hausman, the Latin saying "caveat emptor" definitely belongs here. These figures are the best information available but they cannot be compared to each other. Definitions of sex crime and of recidivism differ from jurisdiction to jurisdiction. They also change from one time to another.

Hausman believes that recidivism rates are difficult to interpret in other ways as well. He explains that cumulative rates always go higher over time because of the way they are compiled. The longer the follow-up period, the higher the rate. The obverse of this is also true, he points out. The longer the sentence a man receives, the less opportunities he has to commit repeated offenses. Another complication is that behavior counted in recidivism is not all antisocial sexual behavior, because new instances of such acts do not all lead to rearrest. The count is further confused because rearrest does not inevitably lead to new charges and not all those charged are convicted. Recidivism is really an inexact concept, but it is the best presently available, Hausman contends.[3]

This answer will not satisfy everyone, but there are few absolutes in dealing with human behavior. Considering the foregoing material, one can better understand why predicting with any certainty how humans will conduct themselves is impossible. The actions of people cannot be put into neat foreseeable categories. We are all affected by the attitudes and circumstances of the society in which we find ourselves.

One sex offender had this to say about that society: "Of course the ideal would be to prevent sex offenses, but I believe that all offenses against society are products of that society. We need to broaden the awareness of the American public and to decide what steps should be taken to prevent the offenses—sexual and otherwise. Our society should be asked to look deep within its social and judicial structures. However, this is an ideal. The reality now is that we are doing almost nothing to help the offender, whether he has committed a sex crime or an armed robbery."

# Part Three

# Sexism, Violence, and the Victim

# 6

# The Effects of a Sexist Society

Sexism and violence permeate our society. Male supremacy is accepted, even expected; domination of women is the norm. Each of us is victimized by and responsible for creating this environment.

A sexist crime is one that is directed at the opposite sex. In the case of sex crimes, this aggression almost always involves a man attacking a woman; because of her weaker image, she is the more vulnerable. This assault is not always physical, however. If a husband refuses to allow his wife to get a job, even though she is qualified, that is psychological rape. If a husband uses his wife's body at will, that, too, is a type of rape.

It is my contention that, given the right conditions, all men have the potential to become sex offenders. Books, movies, television, and advertising all reinforce these attitudes. Sexist behavior is encouraged at all levels of our society.

Maureen Saylor, a therapist supervisor at the Western State Hospital Treatment Program, agrees that a significant number of men are potential sex offenders. "The greater their belief in male supremacy, the more likely they are to be offenders," she claims. A counselor at a rape center in Chicago expressed it this way: "Rape is the logical consequence of the way men and women are taught to treat each other. Boys learn at an early age that aggression and violence prove virility and masculinity, while girls learn to play hard-to-get." The founder of the Center for Rape Concern in Philadelphia says that this behavior perpetuates a "rape society."

One environment that seems particularly to perpetuate sexist attitudes is the armed services. A number of sex offenders told me that their sexism was reinforced in the military: "The service supported my attitudes about women—putting them down—that all they were good for was sex," one rapist told me. "We had a contest that involved what we called a hog board. Pictures of our best-looking girlfriends that were sent to us from home were pinned up on the board. We called the women hogs. The drill sergeant decided who had the best-looking hog, and that guy didn't have to go out for calisthenics that day. As the mail came in, the sergeant would feel a letter to determine if it contained a picture. If it did, he'd remove it, rub it on his crotch, and say, 'Looks like a good hog—get that hog on the board!' And rape wasn't a big deal at all. Women were just something to be screwed anyway."

The charge of potential sex offender is almost impossible for most men to accept, however. They think of the rapist as someone with whom they could never identify in any respect. We witnessed this kind of shielding from the truth when we (the Minneapolis branch of the American Association of University Women) conducted our community symposia on sex offenders. Few men were in attendance. At each event there was a talk on sexism which clearly expressed many of the positions stated here. At the discussion groups which followed, some of the brave men who came were honestly shaken. For the first time they realized that they were not immune from the feelings of sexual assault.

*

The interviews that follow were conducted after the production of some playlets on the subject of rape. A rape crisis center had sponsored these playlets for the benefit of a group of mentally retarded adults. The center wanted to sensitize them to possible compromising positions. I interviewed the four young actors and actresses involved because I was curious to know how they were affected by the rape scenes. Rachel and Norm are married to each other. Sara and Greg are sister and brother. Sara was an actual rape victim.

Rachel told me that when she was first asked to be the rape victim in the play she did not think it would bother her at all. It turned out to be quite the opposite. The first time the cast went through the sketch, it was a terrifying experience. Despite her close relationship with the other members of the cast, Rachel no longer recognized who they were or what the situation was. Her feeling of being trapped became a gut-level response to kick and get away. She put teeth marks on her husband's arm and some scratches and bruises on his scalp. She couldn't help it, she said—they had her pinned. It was not until they had gone through the scenes several times that she was able to objectify the experience.

When they were trying to decide who was going to assume what role, Sara's first thought was: "Well, God, I was not going to be the victim because I had been raped once. I knew this was just playing but I couldn't go through that again." So, in the playlet, she was the person that got away.

It was still real to Sara to watch, however. Though she knew all the time that she was going to escape and that her brother was going to let her, it still was a frightening experience. At one point during rehearsal, the police came in because of the commotion and screaming. This made the situation seem even more authentic.

Greg said he was the first one contacted about doing the performance. The staff at the rape crisis center first had tried to dramatize it themselves, but they were unable to—

not because it was beyond them theatrically or technically—
but because it was too upsetting. When they related their
reaction to Greg, he thought, "Well, sure, that's understandable; they're not theater people." But once he started re-
hearsing, Greg was really aghast at how easy the acting was.
He felt he knew just what to do, and afterward that really
upset him. The part was not at all difficult to play. He felt
as though society had taught him very well—that he had
cues all around him as to how he should behave.

Greg explained that in trying to better understand a character, he usually finds something about it to which he can
personally relate. Since performing this playlet, he thinks
that every man has the rapist potential within him. He had
never acted out a rape before, and to find that those emotions were so close to the surface was frightening. He expressed it this way: "I've thought about it since and I don't
know what to say except that it's there and it's ugly."

Norm agreed with him: "I felt a strong emotional instinct
toward violence which seemed human and easy to draw
on." He said he wanted to talk about the play to people—to
say "Hey, we're doing this rape scene and I'm having to deal
with these emotions and they're ugly and I feel awful, and I
can do it too easily and I don't understand . . . ."

Norm has conducted men's consciousness-raising groups.
One of the questions that they have dealt with is: "What do
we have within us that makes us violent toward each other?
What makes this our way of interacting? How do we get rid
of it?" People often ask if he thinks men's groups do help
prevent sex crimes. Norm said that he hopes they do but he
thinks it is a really slow process, that there is no instant cure.

From the experience of doing the play, Norm was surprised to find how close to the surface the rapist in him is.
"I'm not saying that all males are hopeless. I'm just saying
that most men under certain conditions have these tendencies and don't know it. I think men are particularly armored
against understanding this characteristic."

*

Everyone agrees that rape is reprehensible, but defining it is often difficult. Our values are mixed up with such myths as: (1) women really like to get roughed up; (2) if women tease and then say "no," they deserve to have sex forced on them; (3) men cannot control themselves sexually beyond a certain point; (4) women enjoy being overpowered; (5) only bad girls get raped.

A defense attorney described to me two different types of rapes. In one instance a woman can be assaulted when walking down the street. The attacker might come out of a dark place, grab her, pull a knife, and then rape her. Then, another time, the attack might be the result of a pickup—for instance, going to a bar for a few drinks. Did the influence of alcohol play a part? Sometimes, this attorney thinks, if you lump all of these components together, it is difficult to come to an intelligent conclusion. In the strict sense of the word, in both examples rape occurred, but the offender was a different type of individual. The person in the bar is not the same as the one roaming the streets.

"The man sharing a drink is somebody who has been influenced by the 'come-on.' Her actions might have been misinterpreted. The fact that a man meets a woman in a bar and invites her to go to his apartment in today's society is almost a green light in the minds of some people, especially if there is excessive drinking."

This attorney's reasoning is debatable, however. Look at the *Mr. Goodbar* murder. Is it really the woman's fault that she was raped? One sex offender I know is asked this question often when he gives talks in his community. The usual question is: "Doesn't the victim tempt rape through her actions?" His answer: "The guy is going to commit rape anyway. It doesn't matter how she's dressed or how she's wiggling."

This same offender told me of a conversation he had had with a police officer. "He was telling me that all rapists should be locked up in prison and never let out." The offender subsequently learned that the policeman had a college-educated wife who wanted to work, and that the husband would not allow it. "I think that is a kind of rape, a psychological rape," he said. "She, too, is a victim. She's a victim of society's oppression of women—making women do women's work—to do what men want them to do. I think basically that is what rape is—an aggressive hostile act. Very few men rape for sex. The purpose is to degrade women—to put them on a lower level for the feeling of power."

I asked an incarcerated rapist how he had felt about his victims while he attacked them. He answered: "I didn't think about them as people at all. They were just there—just hate objects. All I thought of was myself and my own anger." Over a period of two years he attacked eleven women and raped six.

Again, describing the nature of rape, "there is nothing sexual about rape," says Karil Ilingbeil, project director of the Sexual Assault Center at Seattle's Harborview Medical Center. "It is a violent act where rather than a gun or a knife, the major weapon is the penis." "Rapists use more than necessary force to reach their goals," says therapist Ralph Garafolo. "Sex is only another weapon they use to humiliate, defile, degrade and gain mastery." "Rape is an outlet for hostilities," says psychologist Geraldine Boozer, who heads the South Florida State Hospital's Sex Offenders Rehabilitation Program. "Rapists have a problem in relating to both men and women, to people in general."[1] It is important to the rapist that he treat his victim as an object; he does not want to know her as a human being.

The late Dr. Joseph J. Peters, director of the Center for Rape Concern in Philadelphia, agreed. "The idea that seductive clothing provokes rape is a middle-class stereotype. If a woman goes out looking sexy, the average sex offender turns the other way. They are not looking for an erotic experience. They are out to attack women in general."

Prisoners Against Rape, the prison-based antirape group in Lorton, Virginia, believes that rape is a product of a patri-

archal culture, an evil which America has
attempt to understand, let alone eliminate
of women, they feel, has its social ori
They believe that criminals, including i
but are created by a society that carries the
social, political, economic and cultural institu
mores, if not in its heart. Hence, again, every man is a p
tential rapist. They point out that several institutions exist
which are geared toward changing the current attitudes of
individual rapists, and that society in general must itself
take the test of reevaluation of attitudes and of understanding repressed emotions. They state in their credo that institutions creating stereotype roles breed backward sexual
attitudes and false consciousness about women. This syste-
matically indoctrinates males into viewing women as being
inferior, as opposed to identifying women as equal social
counterparts. This must be radically changed.

Sexism hurts women; it also hurts men. Certainly the way
we "expect" men to behave is not fair to them either. Few
can measure up to their own and societies' image of what is
a "real man." The rapist exemplifies the extreme case.

# Who Are the Victims of Rape?

The Federal Bureau of Investigation reports that rape is the fastest growing of the nation's most violent crimes. According to *Newsweek*, "Incidents of rape jumped by 9 percent last year [1975], 165 percent in the past fifteen years—and it is estimated that at least three rapes occur for every one reported. By comparison, murder and aggravated assault have risen by about 91 and 142 percent since 1960."[1] Independent criminologists add the important footnote that there are four to ten times as many rapes committed as reported, and that only a small percentage of reported violations end in convictions.

Although the FBI figures do not fully measure the extent of rape today, there is little doubt that the trend is upward. According to the National Commission on the Causes and Prevention of Violence (1969), the rise in rape is part of a general increase in violent behavior in the United States and is largely the result of decaying conditions in urban areas.[2]

While we immediately consider the assaulted woman as the obvious victim of rape, there are many others adversely affected. Parents of the sex offender feel guilty and are often ostracized; those of the offended are angry, hurt, and sometimes suspicious that she may have somehow encouraged the rape. Brothers and sisters of both participants suffer humiliation and so do the spouses and children, especially those of the offender. (One young mother told me that she dreaded the time when her youngsters would be targets of scorn from their contemporaries. How would they explain a father in prison for rape?) Few marriages survive; prisons are called divorce mills.

Society teaches us that rape—especially child molestation—is the most heinous of crimes; even murder is more understandable. Many people can identify with the urge to murder, but not to rape. Though it is essentially a crime of violence, not sex, assaulted women are usually more damaged psychologically than physically. According to Maureen Saylor, this statement is true because of the way in which women look at themselves sexually. If in their own eyes and in the eyes of their families they have lost their pure image—the harm can be great. It is often difficult for them to find support.

While I was researching sex-offender treatment programs, I had the opportunity to meet many victims of rape and talk with them about their experiences. One rape victim, Sharon, told me about her assault and what happened to her afterward. She at present is a college student, has two small children, and lives on welfare. Her marriage has dissolved.

Sharon was raped when she was working as a rental agent for apartment hunters. "Early one morning, a young man came looking for housing. The possible danger of showing an apartment during the day and using my own living room as an office had not occurred to me. The man decided that he wanted the place, and started to fill out the forms. As I talked with him, I had no bad feelings at all. After the application was completed, and I was reading through the information—where he was working, where he was living—he came over behind me and said he didn't understand one question.

"I was playing with my little boy on the floor. When I turned around and looked at him, all of a sudden I got a feeling I'd never had before—I couldn't identify it at the time. Explaining the question didn't seem to satisfy him, and he claimed he still didn't understand. Then I knew that something was wrong, because the terms of the lease were perfectly clear.

"Suddenly he put his hand over my mouth really hard and said, 'You do what I ask and you'll be all right—and shut up!' He kept it there for a little while, and my own strength surprised me because I was able to push his hand away.

"I asked him what he wanted. Since there was a lot of rent money in the desk, I thought at first he might rob me. He covered my mouth again and said, 'I told you to shut up and do what I say!' I managed to ask again, 'What do you want?' 'I want to make love to you,' he said. 'What about my little boy—can I put him to bed?' He kept interrupting me with 'Just don't do anything, just come with me. Do what I say, and you'll be all right.' Again I asked him to let me put my baby in his crib. This time he agreed, and grabbed me very tightly by the arm while I got the baby settled.

"There was no weapon in sight, but he was very scared and very angry. I could tell there were a lot of things going on in his mind and that we weren't functioning at the same level at all.

"After that, he dragged me into the bedroom and threw me onto the bed. He was gentle throughout the rape. He kept asking me for responses. He wanted me to tell him how much I enjoyed it and how good he was—that he was better than my husband. I certainly did say so with no hesitation at all. I knew that that was what he wanted to hear.

"All I was thinking about was getting out of it alive. Then right in the middle of it, I started crying, and he slapped me in the face really hard. He said, 'Don't cry. You know nothing is going to happen to you. You're going to be all right. Just do what I say.' Finally, he got up, and started toward the door. Then he said, 'I don't want you to tell anyone about this, or I'll be back. I'm sorry if I hurt you. I didn't mean to hurt you at all. You just turned me on standing there.' Then he opened the door and left.

"I didn't call the police the day I was raped. After the guy left, I just started crying and crying. I took a shower and took the sheets off the bed, because the man had crabs. Then it was like I was in shock. I started vacuuming the buildings and tried to keep busy. Some people came over, and I told them I was doing caretakers' stuff. I didn't want to tell anyone about what had happened.

"It was kind of strange that the night before, my husband and I had talked about what I would do if I was ever raped. We made plans of action that I was going to use—like hitting him in the eyes, squirting lemon juice, kicking him, or shitting on the bed. But it was all so different and distant from me at the time. The possibility of me really being raped just never occurred to me.

"My husband called me the evening of the rape. I hadn't tried to reach him. He was very angry about the news and came right home. His first feelings were that he wanted to go out and kill the man. All the information on the application was false. He wanted me to call the police immediately, and then to go to the hospital for tests. When I finally did, the police tended to be judgmental because of my having waited for a day. They couldn't understand why. The terms 'alleged victim,' 'alleged attack,' 'alleged' this and that, made me think they doubted my story.

"I later learned that about fifteen rapes were committed in the neighborhood, but that no one had been caught."

Sharon told me about the changes in herself, and the changes that occurred in her relationship to her husband. "Our relationship was strained for a while—it definitely was. Especially sexually, but in other ways too. I wasn't afraid of him, but there were a lot of flashbacks when we were in bed together. Little things that he did would all of a sudden bring back the rape. This was hard for him to understand.

"I made lots of demands on him, like walking me out to the car, meeting me when I came home. I never wanted to go out at night alone, not even next door. My husband started getting really angry about having to do all these things. He just couldn't understand the fear. This went on about three months, and then I kind of worked things out within myself without getting any counseling. I made real efforts to go out at night, and to do things that really scared me."

Sharon said that she didn't feel angry after the rape, but hurt and singled out. "Why did he pick on me as his victim? I guess after I got thinking about it, talking to my husband and a few friends, their angry feedback made my anger start coming out. I felt that I really wanted him caught. But it wasn't for personal satisfaction or good feeling; I was thinking about other possible victims. I warned the women in the neighborhood to be careful. I started getting really angry that this man was raping women. He was so smooth and good at it, leaving no clues at all.

"I was limited socially for a while and didn't want to go out by myself. After the rape, I tended to look at all men as potential rapists. I still have some of that feeling. My husband got tired of hearing about how scared I was and I believe that the aftereffects of the rape contributed to our divorce."

Since Sharon was raped, she has become involved in treatment for both attacked women and sex offenders. "In talking to people on the subject, I find them ignorant and judgmental," she told me. "They are not really aware of what rape is, and what victims go through afterward. I hope to give them a better understanding." This experience is helpful in working out her own problems. She volunteers as a counselor at an urban rape-crisis center, which acts mainly as a twenty-four-hour telephone counseling service for victims of sexual assault. Sometimes she accompanies victims to the hospital and assists them in dealing with the police and the courts.

At an outpatient clinic, she counsels sex offenders. "Because I was raped, I try to give them some insight as to the sort of feelings women have after being sexually attacked. I don't think the men are aware of the trauma until they can hear it from a woman herself," she said.

Sharon explained her attitude about the man who raped her. "Obviously he was in need of some sort of counseling and therapeutic treatment to correct his behavior patterns. He was certainly a danger to other women in the community and himself. I could tell by the look in his eyes that he was really terrified.

"I strongly support treatment for sex offenders and believe that imprisonment alone means confinement and punishment only. Some confinement is necessary, along with treatment, so that while the men are going through the treatment program they are not a danger to society. There should be different sorts of help for the various categories of sex offenders," she feels. "The men must be made aware of, and come to believe, that the behaviors they have been using are inappropriate because of their violent aspect. I think that they should be required to finish the treatment program; only then can an assessment be made to determine when they are ready for returning to the community."

Molly, another rape victim, also shared her experience with me. Until her attack, she said, she thought rape took place only in the dark. She was raped walking on her way to work one early summer evening.

"I worked close to where I lived," she said. "It was starting to sprinkle and I was walking really fast because I didn't want to get wet. I noticed somebody walking on the other side of the street, but I didn't pay much attention. I was walking on the side of the street where the houses were. As I got up almost to the first house, practically to the front yard, somebody grabbed me from behind. I screamed my head off—terrified. I thought 'What's happening here?' The next thing I knew, I felt something go past my face, and a voice said, 'I have a knife. You had better close your mouth.' I still yelled a little bit—that was just reaction, I think—until I felt it really was a knife. Then I shut up. He dragged me across the street to a business that had a service door back off the sidewalk a good ways. He half dragged me, half coerced me by saying, 'If you don't walk, I'll cut your throat.' I was terrified.

"I wasn't about to argue with him. 'Are you going to do this or not?' The only thing I thought about was, 'Okay, he's going to kill me.' I really didn't know at the time what he wanted from me. I kept thinking, 'If he's going to rob me he will kill me because I don't have any money.' Then he started telling me he was sorry. I was crying and begging him, 'Why are you doing this to me, I haven't done anything to you.' You know—'Why me?' My mind was just racing, trying to think of what would be the best thing to do, the right thing to say. Should I shut my mouth? Should I scream again? What should I do? Then he started to apologize and tell me, 'I don't want to hurt you' and 'Please don't—don't try to run, don't scream.' He was almost crying. I'm sobbing.

"He was obviously very, very nervous. Very emotional. He really seemed to be sorry that he was doing this to me. When he started to say 'I'm sorry!' I think I said, 'Then why don't you just let me leave here and nobody will ever know.' Then he told me to lie down and I said, 'No, no!' I cried some more, talked some more, and finally he shoved me down. He started pulling at my clothes, and the more I cried the more reluctant he seemed, but on the other hand he didn't stop.

"Through the whole experience he just kept telling me, 'Please don't make me hurt you. I don't want to hurt you.' But he never took the knife away from my throat. At one point he said, 'I'll put it down over in the grass if you'll promise not to scream.' And I said, 'I promise, I promise I won't scream—put it down!' But he didn't. And it seemed like the longer this went on (it was a very short experience—I don't know how long it was—it seemed like a century at the time, but it probably wasn't more than ten or fifteen minutes), he just kept on appologizing. However, he went right ahead with the rape. At the time I was only afraid for my life. That's the only thing that frightened me.

"I guess that I really didn't realize right up to the moment that he started tearing my clothes off, or tearing at my clothes, that he really was going to rape me. The only thing I could think about was, 'I've got to live to walk away from this.' Afterward, of course, I had a lot of thoughts about maybe I should have reacted differently, maybe I should have kept screaming."

Molly told me that at the time of the rape she wasn't really conscious of what was happening. When she got to the hospital she wasn't sure that the rapist had penetrated her. "He wasn't that brutal with me," she said, "other than bruising me in a few places around the neck and on the arms where he had pulled me around.

"After it was over, he got up and said again, 'I'm sorry, I'm really sorry.' I had gone through this business about, 'I have children, you can't do this to me!' He said, 'Forget about this—you're a nice girl. I'll just go away and you forget about it.' And he ran. I heard him running away, but I was afraid to move. I didn't know whether to get up and run myself, because I kept thinking, 'He's waiting right around the corner of that building. He's still got that knife and he's still going to get me.' Well, I don't know how long I was there—it couldn't have been more than a minute or so before I decided, 'If he wants you that bad, he'll come back and get you,' and I ran.

"I didn't go to the house across the street where there were lights because I had done a fair amount of screaming and no one had come out to help. I really thought there was a possibility that those people had heard. Also, it was very close to where it had all happened and I didn't feel safe.

"I ran the rest of the way to work. Of course, as soon as I came in the door everybody knew what had happened. It must have been written all over my face. The first thing that the fellow I worked with said was, 'Let me call the police.' I sort of tried to compose myself, to get my clothes back together. The police came very shortly thereafter. They told me they had to take me to the hospital. They didn't ask any questions because there were other people around. They took me to the scene where it happened; we went back to look for the knife, but by this time it was dark and we didn't find it."

Molly's treatment by the police was kind. Many rape victims aren't as fortunate. The police didn't interrogate her unduly, but asked only essential questions for making their report. They offered to call her husband, but she wanted him to hear her voice.

Molly's husband admitted to her that he had mixed reactions after learning of the attack—that he went from thinking "If I catch him, I'll kill him!" to "She must have been doing something wrong." "By the time he got to the hospital, the initial shock had passed," she said. "The only thing he said was, 'You're alive, you're not hurt. Thank God!' He was sympathetic. He never had that 'yuk' attitude . . . 'you're dirty, I'm clean.'

"Of course I had to repeat my story to the doctor who gave me the VD test, and again to another doctor when I returned for the results. The police showed me lots of mug shots, but I could not positively identify my attacker. I knew that mistaken identification would be especially serious for a man with a previous record.

"My close friends who knew about the rape were very sympathetic. All of the women were terrified for a while after that—suddenly it hit very close. They thought that it could happen to them. Acquaintances, and people I worked with, had mixed reactions. Many strange remarks were made, like 'How could you stand it? I'd never get over it.

Did they catch him?' Like that would make it all right. Some asked, 'Was he black?' Like if he'd been black, it would have been worse. Some had the 'you're unclean' feeling toward me."

Molly was surprised to learn that women more than men were suspicious about her role in the rape. This is not unlike the way some policemen and hospital attendants often feel. "If they are convinced that the woman was doing nothing to compromise herself, as in my case, then they'll be nice," she observed, "but if they suspect she probably was asking for it, they're not so kind. It's a silly attitude, because no one is ever asking to be raped under any circumstances. If women hitchhike, they should be aware of the risk. If walking on the street in daylight is dangerous, I'm willing to take that chance."

Afterward Molly felt sorry for herself and her attacker, too. "I'm convinced that he could not help doing what he did. I used to think that rape was done for pleasure. Now I know that rapists work out their frustrations by attacking women. I don't think a sex offender is born a sex offender. I don't think a mugger is born a mugger. I think that it's the whole environment that we live in. I know people who have been mugged, for instance, who say, 'That's it . . . from now on I'm carrying a gun!' We're all a part of the same violent environment, where the supposed solution is to go out and take revenge. Watch television, that's all you see. If you've got something working on you, go out and beat somebody up or go out and shoot someone. Hold up a liquor store, rape, or whatever.

"I think that in an ideal society you should be able to come and go as you wish. The fact of the matter is, this is not an ideal society. And if you take the attitude 'I have the right to do anything I want to,' then you're putting the responsibility on somebody else to make sure no harm comes to you. For instance, it would be stupid to leave all my doors unlocked and expect a neighborhood burglar to miss my house. I don't think we should have the attitude 'Well, I have the right for it not to happen to me, so it won't.'

"I come right out and tell people if I think they're doing something stupid. I think the responsibility is ours to protect ourselves wherever possible."

Another victim, Louise, was a happy woman before she was raped. Her intelligence, her pretty face and svelte, graceful figure attracted both men and women. She had an interesting job working as a researcher for a large corporation, and lived in a comfortable, ground-floor apartment. She never thought about rape; it was something that happened to other people. Someone had given her a pamphlet called *What To Do If Faced With the Threat of Rape*—"Be aggressive! Gouge his eyes out! Kick him in the groin!"—but these were just words to her.

Louise had a boyfriend who visited her almost every night. Recently, he had developed an annoying habit—he would ring the bell, then crouch down out of sight, and as the door opened, he would jump up to surprise her. It was a game for him, but Louise did not like it and told him so. On this particular evening, at the sound of the ring, she peered out the peephole and saw only a leather sleeve. "Here he goes again with the dumb stuff!" she thought. "I'm really going to tell him off this time!" Since her friend often wore a similar jacket, she did not question the identity of her visitor. Yanking the door open, ready to yell at him, she froze. It was not her friend. She had hardly a chance to look at the strange man before he extended his arm and pushed her back into the apartment. "Don't say nothin' or I'll slit your throat!" he said as he brandished a knife. He threw her on the floor, ripped off her pants and his own as well. The penetration was quick and easy. Louise wasn't a virgin. Her rapist was physically filthy, and now her body shared his rank, pungent odor. Nausea overcame her; he followed her into the bathroom, where she vomited. Surely he would leave as quickly as he came! But no—he was hungry and demanded something to eat.

He trailed her into the kitchen, holding the knife so close to her back that she could almost feel the point. What could she fix for him? A peanut butter sandwich seemed the quickest and easiest. As she took the knife from the drawer, her hand shook so that she dropped it on the floor. The noise startled her attacker and he almost dropped his weapon. Grabbing the food, he stuffed his mouth, and demanded more—with milk to wash it down. Nausea overtook her again as she watched him eat and smear the remains across his face with the back of his hand. Would he never leave? He shoved her into a chair. A strange numbness overtook her, and she became more like an observer than a participant.

The rapist sat down and started talking about himself. He told her he was from the south and was one of twelve children—none of whom could read or write. He said he needed women, but feared rejection—that the fear made him hate them and himself as well. His only satisfaction came in forced sex.

He had heard the Bible read in church, he said, and he commanded Louise to read some of his favorite passages. As he listened, he wept. She glanced at the clock—he had been there two hours! All the while she was torn between sympathy and revulsion. When he finally left, her first impulse was to take a bath, but no, she remembered a rape prevention pamphlet she had read which said, "Call the police. Don't remove the evidence with soap and water." So she called the police and waited.

Shortly after the officers came, her boyfriend arrived. She sensed that none of them seemed entirely convinced that she was telling the truth. There were no bodily injuries, and no signs of struggle. And why had she let him stay so long? They made her feel guilty and ashamed. Could she possibly have handled it differently? she thought. Finally, after a trip to the hospital for an examination and tests, she was able to remove her filthy clothes and take a bath.

Louise didn't call friends or family that night or the next day. She was confused and shocked almost to the point of being paralyzed. The following night at about the same hour, a face appeared at her window. It was the rapist! She grabbed the phone, and called the police, who arrived in time to arrest him. He was frisked and they found two thousand dollars in his billfold. Of course the police insisted he had stolen the money, even though he protested. The man contended that, because of her kindness to him, he thought he had at last attracted a woman. The money was his total savings as a day laborer which he had taken from the bank to prove his financial success to Louise. The bank verified the withdrawal; the man admitted to the rape, and he was sentenced to zero to thirty years in the state prison.

During the next few weeks, the more Louise thought about the rape, the more compassionate she became. Her rapist was a born loser, she reasoned; no wonder he was so angry and frustrated. At times she regretted having reported the attack and even considered visiting him; he had always been imprisoned in poverty and ignorance—what he needed now was help. She began counseling with other rape victims at a rape-crisis center and working with the police department in sensitivity training. These activities seemed to be therapeutic for her.

I first met Louise six months after the assault, when she spoke at a rape symposium in California. Because of her unique point of view and willingness to speak, she appeared often on radio and TV shows. Soon she became known as "that woman who was raped." We communicated regularly for a while, then I did not hear from her for several months. The next time I saw her she appeared on TV. She had changed. Her hair was cropped short—not carefully coiffed, but chopped out in hunks as if she wanted to get rid of it.

Torn-off jeans and a tankshirt covered her fat, flabby body. The corners of her mouth turned down, accenting a face pocked with blemishes. And what was she saying? "Rapists are animals; they should be locked up forever. Women, band together in vigilante groups and scare hell out of the bastards!"

I immediately wrote to her and she told me her story. She said that since we last had talked, lots of things had changed—she had lost her job and friends, including her boyfriend. She had thought that by speaking out, she could help herself and others, too. The urge to understand her rapist's motivation had seemed to remove some of her own guilt feelings. Her new life took so much energy there was little left for her work, however. She naively figured that her boyfriend and others would understand. She should have known that he'd hate the rape publicity and be embarrassed by her empathetic attitude, she wrote.

Louise further wrote that she had been ostracized after the rape. "Women really avoid me," she said. "It's as if I have a disease they don't want to catch—the disease of having been raped. I feel I was abused twice, first by the man and then by everyone else. Now I seem to hate everybody—my friends, the rapist, and myself. Why did it happen to me? What did I do wrong? Could I have prevented it? My life seems ruined and all because of something I couldn't help—or could I? Will I ever know?"

The reactions that friends and family have toward the victim make a huge difference in whether or not the victim can cope. In Louise's case, these reactions were most destructive. In the case of Terry, the attitude of her family was very important. It shows that psychological damage need not always be irreparable.

Terry was ten years old when she was raped. It is estimated that one in six girls will be molested before the age of sixteen. Children are popular targets because they are less inhibited and more trusting. Terry told me how the rape occurred. She and her girlfriend had been skating at the neighborhood rink, which was maybe six or eight blocks from her home. It was an evening in January, the ice was perfect, and they had skated while waiting for one of their parents to pick them up and take them home. For some reason, the parent was delayed.

Terry decided to change into her boots because of the cold, and she went into the bathroom, which was outdoors. To her surprise, a boy lunged at her from behind the bathroom door, cornered her, and then ran away. Terry immediately became afraid and ran outside wearing one boot and one skate. In the meantime the boy changed his mind and ran back toward her. He, of course, had an advantage because he wore shoes and he was bigger and stronger. There was a very high bank of ice down which Terry slid on her one skate. The boy chased her, threw her onto the ground, and then ran away again.

"He was kind of rough with me," Terry said. "I think he was upset because I had hit him in the face with my skate. I just kept pleading with him not to hurt me and told him I would do anything he wanted. He was real confused and didn't seem to know what he wanted to do. Again he ran away and as I was getting up he came back and said he wanted to do more. That's when he raped me.

"I screamed for my girlfriend to run. I was so little and the boy was so big, of course he hurt me. I could feel the blood running down my leg. But he kept right on till he finished, even though I was sobbing. He told me that he would kill me if I told anyone.

"My girlfriend, who had gotten away, called my parents. My dad was outraged. He wanted me to ride around the city and find this man or boy. At the time I wasn't really sure I could identify him because it was dark when I was raped.

"My mother told me that I must feel very sorry for this

person because he was sick. She kept telling me that I had a lot of presence of mind for a little girl, so I think the whole perspective I always kept was that the situation was unfortunate. I wouldn't want it to happen to anyone else. I felt there was something wrong with the boy—I guess because my mother had explained that to me and because the police were drawn into it. It all seemed very official. I was told it was not my fault, but was just something that occurred in life.

"My parents and I talked about it later. It's scary and somehow reassuring at the same time that even as a child you don't have to be told—you instinctively know somehow what's happening and how to deal with it. I knew I was going to be raped. It wasn't like being chased by a playmate. He had something very bad for me in his mind and I knew that he couldn't help himself.

"It was clear to me how frightening it must have been for my girlfriend, who had to run away, and what a difficult decision she had to make. She was only ten, too. I knew she had to get away—she knew it too, and I had to give in to the rapist."

Terry didn't recognize the rapist. He was a teenager who lived in her neighborhood, but he went to a different school. Terry later learned that she wasn't his only victim; he had molested, threatened to kill, and raped several young girls before he was finally caught.

For a long time Terry wouldn't go anywhere without her father. She made him put extra locks on the doors. She was afraid to go to school. She was afraid of being teased and taunted by schoolmates. "It's taken me a long time to fully be comfortable with saying to someone that I was raped," she explained. "Not until I was in college and meeting new people and the subject of rape would come up did I have the courage to say, 'Well, I was raped.' At first I did it for the shock value because people would just say 'Huh? No!' They would look at me like—well, it's really strange. The reactions were that of shock, but I was never sure what they really thought."

Terry's brother told how he reacted to his sister's rape: "When we got the call from her friend and went down to find her, I was fully of the same mind as my father. I had picked up a wrench or something on the way out of the house. When we found my sister, my mother took care of her while my father and I searched the area around the skating rink. If I had found him, I'm sure I would have killed him if I could. I was really angry and feeling blood, you know. That's not like me ordinarily and it's not like me now." He expressed his present feelings toward rape: "I've interrupted several rapes since my sister's attack. I've just happened to hear someone scream and have been able to rescue the women. I think that a lot more of it goes on than people realize. They simply tune out a lot of the sounds at night. I happen to be tuned in because of my sister's experience.

"Rapists are really unsure of themselves. I know that some rapes are planned, but many times determined resistance or opposition can frighten the rapist away. I think they try to pick people that they're sure will be weaker.

"I have some sympathy for the position of the rapist. Stories I've heard from offenders I've met is that it's just something that kind of came up right then. Most of them don't plan long in advance until they are successful a time or two—the first time is almost accidental for most people. Hearing about their sex histories and what their total lives were like, I could understand why they might rape. People tend to beat on those weaker than themselves when they've been beaten on by somebody stronger. It seems to be the classic pattern. People who are that frustrated in their sexual lives, and at the same time have a feeling of powerlessness, take it out on someone else who seems even less powerful."

Terry's brother thinks that the initial act may not be

learned behavior—that the offenders have probably never seen a rape, but the aggression and the propriety of using aggression toward women, who are weaker, has been ingrained in our culture. It is another way of dominating. "If we can somehow undo the domination trips that males are programmed into, and I think it is programmed, not biological, I think that might help. I see men's liberation as a means of doing that. How, specifically, I can't say. Early sex education is essential because it's difficult at age thirty-five to change a person's whole way of thinking."

Perhaps the ideal place for sex education is in the home. However, all parents cannot be relied upon to communicate accurate information on the subject of sex. It appears to me that schoolteachers especially trained in this area are the best qualified for the job.

Of course the immediate victim of rape is by no means the only victim, as we have seen. Families and friends of the offender also are victimized.

I talked with Nancy, the wife of a sex offender, to find out what effects her husband's behavior had had on her and their children. She told me that since her husband's incarceration she and their two children, aged two and four, have lived on welfare. She is a pleasant woman in her twenties, with long blond hair and an easy smile. The children often ask where their father lives and she tells them that he was naughty and therefore has to work away from home. As they grow older, she knows this answer will not satisfy them. In order to stretch her check, she was living with her parents at the time of this interview. "Both my father and mother believe my husband should be locked up for the rest of his life. They can't understand why I won't divorce him," Nancy explained.

"I was brought up in a rigid mother-dominated family. My brother, sister and I felt secure and well cared for but didn't see my father much because he worked nights and slept days. Mother made all the decisions, so I considered her the head of the household. My father just earned the money. I behaved the same way after I was married. My husband never complained about me being bossy, but I know now that I really bugged him.

"I first knew that he was a rapist when the police came to our home and arrested him. I didn't believe it until he called me from the police station and admitted he was guilty.

"I thought our marriage wasn't much different from other marriages that I saw. My husband was a warm, understanding, kind, wonderful man, and an exceptional father. He always had time to be with our daughter.

"About the time of his arrest he had a couple of bad breaks. The place where he worked was a dead-end street for him. He was just stagnant and it dragged him down. I was no help either. Because of two miscarriages within a year all I could think of was myself. I thought, 'Am I ever going to have another baby?' My attitude with him was 'You take care of yourself, I'll take care of myself.' We never sat down and talked about our problems as I know we should have. Of course, my husband couldn't tell me all of his.

"After the rapes I didn't see any change in his personality. (Of course I didn't know about them.) I guess he actually blocked that part of his life out of his mind. Maybe he had to, otherwise he couldn't have lived with himself. He sort of lived with two personalities, in almost two different worlds—one as a rapist, and the other as a father and husband. He told me later that after each rape it was like, 'I'll never do that again—I'm okay now.' I knew he drank but didn't realize he was becoming an alcoholic. The assaults took place when he had been drinking, but he never abused me."

Nancy's husband had committed two rapes but was charged with only one. When he discovered that an innocent man had been identified as the person committing the first offense, he pleaded guilty to that crime as well. "This took a lot of courage because committing two rapes is much more serious than one," Nancy delcared. I asked her how people reacted after he was arrested. "They wanted to know mainly what had happened to him. They couldn't understand it. They were really sympathetic but it was very hard for me to talk to them."

Her husband was out on bond for nine months and during that time they were in therapy. "We went every week for about three or four months. We went alone, just the two of us. The type of sessions were good because we weren't communicating about anything serious.

"Sexual problems were hard for us to discuss all our married life. When we first started therapy, we sat knee to knee and practically nose to nose and talked to each other. The psychiatrist would say, 'Well, how does that make you feel? Are you angry? Are you sad?' I had a problem with those questions because my parents are very unemotional. They never showed their feelings and neither did I. We didn't kiss and hug. Us kids were taught that you just didn't cry in front of people. My feelings were always kept down so this kind of therapy was really difficult for me.

"We paid for the treatment by borrowing money from friends and relatives. I worked as a typist for about three or four months after the arrest. Finally my husband found a job, but lied about having been arrested. After he had worked for three or four weeks, he went to his boss and told him the truth, and he was fired.

"So then he found another job. I'm telling you, it was really tough, because every job he applied for, he told them, 'I'm out on bond for rape.' He finally found work, but the problem was that he wanted to be home as well as at work. Spending as much time as possible with me and the children was too important to him. His mind wasn't on the job so he finally was fired.

"He knew he would be sent somewhere, somewhere away

from home. What our attorney was trying for was a year in the workhouse, with a work release, so he could continue with his treatment. Of course, the judge wouldn't go along with this, since you can only be in the workhouse for one year. The judge felt that a year wasn't enough treatment time, so he had to go to prison."

A close marriage relationship is difficult for them to maintain. His indeterminate sentence is zero to thirty years. Whether or not they will be able to pick up the pieces and live together again is a constant concern for them both.

# 8

# The Special Case of Incest

Maggie is twenty-three years old; a tall, slender, pretty red-head. She was the victim of an incestuous relationship with her father from age six to age fifteen—a relationship that damaged her entire life. As a child she did not understand what her father was doing. She told me about her experience:

"My father came into my room and I would think that I was dreaming. And the next day, when asked about it, he said, 'It was a dream.' At first I'd wake up just as he'd be leaving the room, and later on I felt him fondling me, touching my breasts and my genitals. There was no intercourse at that time." She spoke of the relationship between her father and mother. "I blamed my father because my mother had so many nervous breakdowns when I was very young. They would physically fight a lot. My father was abusive to her. She kept saying that she was going to leave him but wanted to wait until us kids got a little older. He was also sexual with my older sister, but I didn't know that until I was fifteen.

"I always thought there was something wrong with the

way my father treated me," Maggie admitted. "He threatened to kill me if I told my mother about our sexual activity and that really scared me. I didn't understand exactly what was wrong, but I got the message that something was really bad. I couldn't talk about it to anyone. When I was about twelve, actual intercourse started. By then I knew what was going on, but to me, the whole thing was my fault. At six years, I thought I should have been old enough to know that I shouldn't let him touch me. Since I didn't try to change anything for so long, I felt responsible. The trouble must be with me and not my father. I also thought that if I told my mother she would have another nervous breakdown and that probably my dad would get so angry I'd have to leave home. If I told anyone, I would lose my family. Having a crappy one was better than none."

Maggie said that at first she used to like the added attention from her father. She felt special and there was some sexual pleasure, too, she admitted. But by age twelve, all the enjoyment ended. "I would want my father to be loving. One time when I brought home my report card, my dad asked me to sit on his lap and show it to him. I wanted him to be fatherly and loving so I did what he asked. He didn't even look at my report card but started being sexual with me. I felt like I had set it up by sitting on his lap—that he thought I wanted to be played with. I felt guilty about leading him on without realizing I had. It got to the point where I felt I shouldn't have any need for him at all—any needs for care, affection, or for even having a father. If I did he always became sexual.

"I learned as a kid to detach myself," she remarked. "To say, 'This isn't really happening, this isn't really going on.' I would lie in bed believing that if I got close to the wall Dad couldn't touch me. And when he still did, I would go into the wall in my mind. I used to look at my dad's being sexual with this little girl who was crying and I'd be outside of her. I learned to say, 'This is not me. This is not my dad. This is not happening.' I'd fantasize that my real father wasn't sexual; he really was a good man—he had to be because he was my father."

Maggie's father came into her room about three or four times a week. She soon learned that if she did not fight with him at night, the experience was less uncomfortable; and too, if she fought, there were penalties later. Punishment for other things was common under those circumstances. She always knew that later trouble resulted from her lack of cooperating sexually. This feeling that women must be sexual with men or they will suffer has carried through her life. For her it was a way of protecting her mother, too.

Maggie told me that from age eleven or twelve, maybe even before, she had started to get into trouble. Running away from home or not coming home at night were common practices. When she was fifteen, she had a juvenile record as a runaway.

Friendships with her contemporaries were difficult—they were in the stage of talking about adolescent thrills, like "I kissed so and so." She was reminded of how different her home was and she felt isolated. The men she chose to be around were all hard, "nothing hurts me" type of people, as she described them. They too had been hurt, so there was a connection between her pain and theirs. She said: "They were all hard-asses. One time at about age twelve, I was walking down the street. A couple of older guys, maybe twenty-three years old, said that they would take me to Virginia, where they lived. I said, 'O.K., let's go!' I thought anything to get away from my family was good. They raped me, and that's all that came of it. I was so vulnerable. By then I was drinking quite heavily and I was pretty well plastered at the time of the rape. The booze came from my older friends. Kids my age I had nothing in common with."

Each time Maggie ran away, she would get punished and grounded. Because in her opinion she was a bad person, the penalties seemed appropriate. "I always told my mother that I hated my father because he punished me," she remembered. "I never told her the real reason.

"When I was fifteen I decided I could live by myself. I ran away to a girlfriend's mother and told her about the relationship with my father. I felt like I just couldn't live at home anymore. The woman called my mother, but she didn't believe the story. I had already gotten into so much trouble that she said it was another one of my tall tales. I'd been trying to get out of the house for the last three years by running away or saying that I wanted to move out. This was another method of getting my way, she said. I know now that when kids tell lies, it's for a reason.

"Mother finally set up a meeting with my father. It was then that my sister admitted he had had sex with her, too. My sister was different than me. She just stayed home and was quiet—never had any friends or went out.

"When my mother first confronted my father, he cried for a long time and said that maybe all he wanted was a little affection. That's as far as he went to admitting the relationships. After that, my mother got a divorce. She said she knew my father was running around with other women, but she never admitted to our sex life."

Maggie's mother later confessed to Maggie that she was afraid of her husband from the day they were married. Her own father had been abusive to her family and left them when she was four years old. Her stepfather beat her, too—that was the only kind of man she had ever known. Finding her husband cruel was not a new experience.

Maggie did not know much about her father's family background except that his father was an alcoholic. Her own father never drank but his compulsive rage often made him appear drunk. Heavy drinking was a part of her mother's life. "I lived with my mother for a while after their divorce and continued to get into trouble. Then I began living in foster homes. Nobody admitted that incest might have damaged me or that that was why I 'acted out.' I felt like such a bad person. The judge that decided on the foster homes didn't ask me any questions and I didn't offer any information. I thought my problems were really brought on by me. Not even my mother had ever said, 'I believe that you are telling the truth, and that this sexual stuff really went on. What did it do to you? How do you feel about it?' My father wouldn't even admit he was being sexual when it was happening."

Although Maggie's delinquency record included promiscuous sexual behavior as well as drunkenness and running away, she rarely even kissed a man, she claimed. Because of her father's possessiveness, she felt almost married to him. Whenever she did invite a boy home, her father would order him out.

She told of her experiences living in foster homes. "I lived in three. One of them was with my dad's sister. She used a lot of stuff against me, you know, about being a delinquent. Because I was a bad girl, I had to come in early. Even though her son was younger, he could stay out later, so I didn't stay there very long. I wasn't a ward of the state; my parents just sort of put me in places until I was about sixteen. They were always in homes of relatives. After age sixteen I had real foster parents, and the family was good to me. They had money, and I got a lot of attention when I was sick and at other times too. At first we got along okay, but later I just didn't know how to deal with the situation. The contrast between them and my family was too great, and yet I'd get real angry at my foster parents for trying to take their place. Nobody could ever replace them, no matter how they behaved. They tried to take away some of the pain my parents had given me, but they couldn't; it was just there and no one could take it away. In a funny sort of way I still have an affection for my father and mother, and I wanted to hold on to it.

"Another thing is that I had tools to deal with only a dysfunctional family. I knew how to handle Dad beating up

Mom or Dad being sexual with me. The feelings were uncomfortable and confusing, but they were all I ever had to work with. People who treated me different were too strange for me. All of my boyfriends were 'hard-ass' guys who behaved somewhat in the way I was used to. Or I chose women who were real weak because they reminded me of my mother. And that's how I see it carrying on from generation to generation."

Maggie lived with foster parents until she moved in with a man at age sixteen. He was an alcoholic and physically abusive to her.

She quit high school before graduating. By then, drugs had taken over her life—speed, acid, and hard drugs, as well as alcohol. She earned money as a prostitute. "I started prostituting at age eighteen. I did it on my own—I'd never have a pimp!" she said with disdain. "I'd go into bars and meet some businessman, older man, who would give me money. I was so disgusted with sex that I didn't get anything from it—I'd learned to not even feel. My whole body was numb, like it wasn't even there. My attitude with men was, 'I'll be sexual with you, but you give me something in return.' The anger I felt for my father came out by screwing those men.

"When I look back now, I think prostituting was the most sane thing I could have done—to get high, to find some escape, to take my anger out on other men—to get some sort of release. Another thing—when I was fifteen, there were three or four social workers that I did tell about the sexual stuff but they didn't do anything. Mom told them her usual story that it was another one of my lies because I didn't tell the truth about anything anyway. I saw one of them just recently. She said that there were so many other family problems, with Mom being nervous and so forth, that she didn't want to deal with my problems. I see incest as the core of everything else I did. The social workers' attitudes didn't help me in my lack of trust for adults. If Mom had really cared, she would have at least listened to me. I began thinking that I was crazy, that I must be wrong in thinking what had happened was so terrible. No one else seemed to care. This is very common with most cases of incest, I have found. We end up feeling like offenders ourselves."

Maggie had no guilt feelings about being a prostitute. People would try to shame her but she felt nothing. She had no conscience.

"I was a prostitute for two years," she continued. "By then I was so strung out on drugs and was shooting them up by then. I wanted to die. I knew I was dependent and couldn't get through a day without the drugs. I had been in psychiatric wards several times before and had told them about the sexual stuff with my family, but they wouldn't listen. They didn't even say I had a problem with drugs. Finally I was referred to a family agency, where I talked to a social worker about everything. She really listened but felt she couldn't do anything about my family problems until I got off drugs. At her suggestion I joined a drug treatment program, where I was an inpatient for six and a half months.

"Oh, another thing I forgot to say was that at seventeen, another social worker put me back at home with my father. I cried and screamed and said I was too scared of him. I hadn't seen him since I was fifteen. This was intended to be a punishment because I wouldn't stay in foster homes. They expected me to behave better when I returned. I was at home for two weeks and then I ran away. My father remarried and he treated his new wife the same as he did my mother. This is another example of how little protection kids have. If a kid leaves a home, and tries to tell somebody why, she should never be sent back to the family. When a girl makes the big decision to tell someone in the first place, she has decided to not live with her family. What she wants is support."

After the inpatient therapy, she was treated for two years in an after-care program. The drugs had helped blot everything out, but now with their effect wearing off, she started to remember her experiences with her father. At the treatment center they wanted her to beat on the pillow to take some of the anger out, but it was difficult because she had suppressed those feelings for so long. Too many tragic happenings were a part of her life. She was raped more than once, but felt guilty for somehow setting up even those situations. Would she never lose those guilt feelings? Unless men were brutal to her, she didn't know how to handle them.

Relating to men in the treatment center was difficult, too. "Because of my past experiences, I had an intuitive pickup on who felt sexual toward me," Maggie explained, "whether they knew it or not. If they touched me, and there was any sexual message at all, I could tell it and would get real angry. Most of the women counselors didn't know how to deal with this incest stuff at all. One I tested by saying things like, 'My father kissed and fondled me,' and then I'd wait to see how she reacted. It shocked her but she did let me talk, so that helped get a lot of that stuff out on the surface. I then remembered what happened. Some of the time I'd get so emotional that I could only cry, and at another time I'd be cold—the way I'd handled the emotional part before was to take drugs. Many incest victims have to learn at an early age to detach themselves from their childhood experiences. To most people their stories are not real."

After leaving the center, Maggie went into family therapy treatment to help with the incest guilt. She was then living alone. She said that her behavior pattern was much the same—still getting picked up, and being propositioned. She did not actually prostitute herself, because her therapists would not allow it, but she still had the desire, and saw no valid reason why she should not. Her counselor said her feelings were natural because of all the anger that was still there. Her drug habit was cured but everything else was the same. Being depressed and unable to get close to anyone was still a part of her personality. Getting at the root of her problem became a must. She was ready for a different kind of treatment.

A psychologist became her private therapist. She admitted that she would deliberately set him up to be sexual with her. "I almost begged him to be," she confessed. "Then I thought I could continue to say, like I always had, that men are all alike and therefore there was no hope for me. I could still fuck over men and still get them going. I wanted to change, but yet it was too painful. Getting respect from men made me more clearly see my father for what he was. I had genuine beliefs that all men were only sexual and abusive. I always picked that kind of man and I believed that no other type existed for me. To not be abused gave me sadness." Her therapist admitted to finding her attractive and she finally understood that this condition is possible without men losing control.

Maggie worked with him for a year and then went into a women's group where the women had many types of difficulties. She was encouraged to fantasize killing her father, which at first terrified her. Later she began to understand that such fantasizing was perfectly normal and right.

At that time, she asked her father to join a therapy group. For six months she called him every other night. She still could not face the truth that she did not have a family. "I had been the crazy one for so long, I wanted him to share the craziness," she confessed. "I was the one getting the help because apparently no one else needed it, I thought. I got tired of protecting everyone. When I talked to my father, he'd say, 'What sexual things? I don't know what you're talking about.' That was what everyone had said all my life. Fortunately I was at a better place with myself and could see things more clearly." Her mother and her sexually abused sister refused therapy as well.

She talked about relating to men. "Incest victims can't

settle for the usual kind of associations. If you've been raised in a sexual environment, sexual intercourse isn't a priority in your man-woman relationships. I've had too much sex all my life. What I want from a man now is some intimacy, closeness and sex, but in that order."

Until recently, stories like Maggie's rarely have been aired in public. The subject of incest has been strictly taboo in our society. Statistics are hard to come by, but as we are gaining more insight, we know that incest, though still quite successfully hidden, is prevalent. The practice cuts across all standards of living, but relatively few cases are reported, especially in the more affluent families. (As one program administrator said, "When the family looks good, it's hard to say that there are problems. If pregnancy occurs it is usually attributed to someone outside the family.") Even when cases are reported, the handling of the information is often inefficient, and detrimental to the child. Unfortunately, there are few treatment centers that deal with incest. Neglect is still the most usual procedure.

Debbie Anderson is the director of the new Sexual Assault Services in Minneapolis, Minnesota. She is trying to modernize the whole organization as it relates to incest victims. She told me some of what she had learned about incest victims and their families:

"We pretty well know now that sexual behavior is learned most often at home. It must be emphasized that children are true victims. They're vulnerable and easy to exploit. Adults have to be responsible or pay a price of sorts, but that doesn't mean the parents should be locked up without any treatment. Their behavior may indicate that they should be in a secure place while receiving the therapy. But kids really have no options when somebody is sexual with them; however, children usually know when they are being used. They don't have to be assaulted in order to be exploited, and they understand what adults mean, even though their parents may deny being coercive.

"Incestuous families stunt the growth of the children, but society doesn't want to recognize what is happening. The whole subject is too painful. We shove the truth under the rug and ignore its presence. The very inner core of the child is meddled with and used. It turns upside-down who is taking care of whom. The children should be the children," Anderson emphasized.

"Since most children initially enjoy sexual sensations, the parents' fondling pleases them," Anderson explained. However, children soon realize that, contrary to their first reaction, the caressing is being done for the parents' satisfaction only. "Sometimes these children get privileges in the family that the other siblings don't. Children need to be parented, not bribed," she added.

The pattern varies in families. Sometimes the relationship is between only one child and the parent, but it can involve more than one. The cases usually seen are between fathers and daughters. "There are few instances reported involving mothers and sons, but mothers can be sexual too," she pointed out. "For instance, they may tickle the boys too much. A fourteen-year-old boy ran away because his mother constantly undressed in front of him. Although his mother was seductive, there were no sexual relations. The son was trying to develop his own sexuality and the person always in his vision was his mother. Most children love their parents and the real horror is that the parents are not caring properly for them.

"We pretty well know that mentally ill people come from situations where they're hearing conflicting messages at one time. This happens with incest," Anderson observed. She used her own children as examples. "If I say, 'Don't get into the cookie jar,' they can tell if I really mean it. But if I say it in such a way that I'm really meaning, 'Be naughty and go ahead,' but when they do I punish them, they know my real intent was to have an excuse to dominate. Here we have some potential trouble. Children get the nonverbal message and the cases of incest are similar."

She thinks that between siblings incest is not serious. Most children want to see what the other looks like. "They're just sexually curious. If, however, the relationship is between a six-year-old girl and her sixteen-year-old brother, that is coercion and serious.

"Sometimes the wife is almost an enabler in an incestuous family. She either knows about what's happening consciously, or has pushed it away so that she doesn't recognize it. Also, if she sees it and tries to remedy the condition, this will mean a struggle with the entire family. Most mothers are scared to turn their families upside-down. If they go to an agency and expose the situation, they may have to financially support the family and might have no work experience. For the most part, the burden is on them to get the family straightened out. I've seen a large number of mothers who allow incest to go on between the fathers and daughters because they themselves have been similarly victimized. It's like the battered child syndrome."

She gave statistics about the county in which she serves. "Since 1963 there have been 1087 instances of kids reported to the welfare department as either battered or sexually abused. There were 6 in 1963 and 290 in 1975. There were 22 police investigations, 28 deaths, and only 8 criminal prosecutions. That's a sad commentary on due process. Where children are concerned, there is none! Countrywide, if a child is being exploited by parents, we as a society in effect have said, 'It's okay.' Each of us has to look at our own children, plus how we were parented. Most people experience some block and pain connected with childhood," Anderson contended. "I find that many individuals deny their upbringing. They entirely lose perspective of themselves as children, forgetting how vulnerable they were."

According to Anderson, 75 percent of the prostitutes encountered in her work had their first sexual experience at home with their fathers. There, sexuality was used to accrue certain gains. Because they were exploited, they victimize others. In most cases, prostitution is not meeting any real needs, but is a way of releasing anger.

"The kids act out and do crazy things to let the community know that something is amiss or a mess in their families. They don't run away and become problems for no reason whatsoever. Sometimes it's difficult and frightening to find out what is causing the behavior. There is too much pain at the base of discovering; it often comes out as anger. The kids who run away and get into drugs are really trying to tell someone, 'My family has a problem.' They're waving a big flag but generally get stoned to death," Anderson related.

She explained the typical procedure that is presently followed in her county. "When a situation is severe enough, if reported, and the Child Protection Agency believes the incident has happened, they'll investigate the case. Where else is a victim treated like this? Just imagine if somebody called up and said, 'My store has been robbed.' Nobody would say, 'Listen, if we believe you, we'll come out and look into it.' It's this way with children because incest has been hidden for so long. Only in the last few years have we admitted that rape really happens. It's sort of an evolution in learning about ourselves.

"In this county's procedure, which is common to most, the social worker assumes the role of policeman, judge, and attorney. She becomes everything. All the decisions are made by her and no treatment is recommended. What has upset the family is severe, and requires intense therapy. We don't expect people to be cured of chemical dependency after a social worker has made a visit or two. Why should incest be treated differently?" Incest, like alcoholism, is a kind of disease, she feels. "We are just now acquiring enough knowledge to isolate it."

Anderson worked in the Child Protection Agency, where there was no outlined procedure for dealing with incest, for seven months. No real criteria were used to determine what constituted a believable case. "Social workers would go to the homes where the complaints have been made, wearing their many hats. They had no arrest or law-enforcement power, even though a felony had been committed. They would say, 'We're here to investigate the case.' Between the arranged visit and the actual encounter, all evidence may have been destroyed."

She cited some examples of convincing documentation: "There was a six-year-old with whom her father was reported to have had oral sodomy. The daughter had thrown up on the rug, which had been taken to the police station for examination. In the vomit, seminal fluid was found. (The girl had complained to her mother, who had called the police.) A sixteen-year-old I worked with had written in her diary after each incestuous incident with her father. It was another way of telling her story and the information was important to the evidence. She also told her school counselor. When her father, who was a policeman, was arrested, he became so upset that he vomited. Incest occurs at all levels of society," Anderson contends.

A prison sentence for the father is not always the best solution, she feels: "Incest disrupts the very inner core of how children's needs are met. A felony has been committed and the offense should remain in that category. Fathers should not always go to jail or even have criminal records. In the case of the six-year-old referred to earlier, her father is in prison because he was excessively abusive to the family. Some families might be better served if the father went to a hotel until due process was completed. Only in unusual cases should the father be sentenced to prison.

"Decisions about what happens to the families are at present made by the welfare department and the cases are brought to juvenile court," Anderson explained. "This is wrong. Adults should be taken to adult courts. In this county, the children are usually whisked from the home immediately, are put into a boarding school, in a temporary foster home, or kept in the juvenile center for a while. Both the father and mother go before the juvenile court, where they just get their wrists slapped; the children pay the price for what has happened.

"The children are eventually sent back to live in the home with the persons who sexually abused them. An assaulted adult would never be forced into a similar situation. Never would we punish the adult and ignore the assailant.

"Families are considered too scary to touch. Children often 'act out' by running away, and therefore have records of delinquency; it is this charge that children are treated for. Few people want to admit that all the behavior stemmed from the incest."

Debbie Anderson would like to have a team of people make the decisions. She contends it is too easy for one agency to get a vested interest. "The constitutional rights of those 1087 kids have been severely violated," she declared. "In years to come they all could have valid court cases."

She thinks that procedures presently used for other rape victims should be set up for victims of incest. "Incest is rape and can be similarly treated. There has been a 43 percent increase in reported adult rapes the past two years, so the system apparently works. I am in the process of organizing my office so that when incest is reported, we will be the initial contact. The police, judges, and attorneys will be called in to work with us. Under the new procedure hospitals will analyze the evidence, because in certain situations the child may need to be hospitalized. Psychological care will be available, especially for the very young. Teenagers should receive a medical evidentiary examination without charge, as do all other victims of rape. After the father is arrested, the possible danger in his returning home will be determined. Each consideration is to be individualized," she said. "Continual support to the family by a social worker is important as well.

"Where more action is needed, the cases will come to the

attention of the county attorney's office to be charged. There is a state statute which provides that the courts have jurisdiction over an offender for one year. If recommended treatment is completed, the criminal record will be erased.

"At present battered children are hospitalized, and nothing but physical help is applied. The police resist investigation because they know that nothing constructive will come of it," she explained. "They may make the situation even worse by showing the family that no one is going to be of any real assistance.

"If the parents are not willing to change, there should be punishment, but most will want to cooperate. An honest effort to make one's self healthier feels good to most people. When one is shamed and belittled, change has little incentive. Incest is presently the most degrading of all felonies, and giving it understanding is going to be difficult for many.

"Because society is becoming enlightened in other sensitive areas, such as alcoholism and mental illness, accepting treatment for incest should come faster. Many more people are molested in their families than we have any notion of, and this procedural change will probably bring skeletons out of the closets," she concluded.

As we have seen, the Santa Clara Treatment Program in San Jose, California, is considered by Edward Brecher to be one of the most successful programs now treating incest victims. It is an outpatient center operating in the Juvenile Protection Parole Department.

"What happens to the children varies," Brecher explained. "It depends on the child. The juvenile probation protection workers do what is necessary in each case. There are several patterns. However, for a significant number of children, there is no need to label them as victims, or to take them out of the setting where they may be functioning effectively. In these cases, it is through therapy with the parents that the child's problems are considered. The parents give each other the kinds of advice needed to maintain decent parent-child relations."

Brecher sat in on one of the center's self-help group sessions; it was devoted to one of the fathers, who raised the question: "Having had sex with my fourteen-year-old daughter for three years, and now having ended it, I am home again, and trying to maintain a decent household. How can I establish a normal relationship of discipline which is clearly separated from my old sexual patterns?" Brecher said that family after family which had faced and solved precisely this problem became involved in the discussion and out of it came considerable insight in how you can shift relations with your children.

The subject of the wife's part in having rebuffed her husband was brought up. Brecher commented: "There are different kinds of situations. The wife who unconsciously encourages an incestuous situation by withdrawing from the husband and closing her eyes to the facts is in no sense a co-conspirator. Then there is the wife who actually wants her husband to have sexual relations with the child. I think the latter kind is rare, even though it is hard to believe that a wife would not know that her husband and daughter had been 'making out,' for as long as seven years in some cases. In any conscious sense she does not know, and certainly needs help."

While a surprising number of husbands and wives stay together during and following the incest experience, he observed, there are divorces. In these cases some husbands with their new women friends stay active in Parents United, a self-help volunteer group. It was even more remarkable to Brecher that wives stay on and continue to participate with their new men friends. These men and women feel very strongly the need for this therapy, even though they have not been in the incestuous situation.

"According to therapists who are experienced in treating incest families, all of them function poorly as a family unit," Brecher said. "One group is strongly family centered. The idea of adultery—going outside of the family for a sex partner—would seem to the husband to be an absolute betrayal and utterly beyond his imagining. Violating God's law and man's law would be an outrageous imposition. The development of a warm, personal, subsequently sexual relationship with one of the children in the family just does not violate this for him."

Brecher continued: "I would like to speak to the other side of this coin, and it's a distressing one. This is the extent to which the spirit of incest—this deep concern with one's own feelings for members of the family—can lead to much strife, bitterness, and rejection within a family. For example, a father may be a damned good father to his daughter at age eight, nine, and ten. She begins to reach sexual maturity, and he becomes vaguely aware of some feelings he has in this area. He finds them very threatening and obnoxious. He reacts by rejecting his daughter completely, becoming harsh and brutal toward her, and staving her off. The daughter thinks that she has lost her father's affection. She may become quite hostile to men generally—not just to her father. The ordinary exchange of affection, of hugs and kisses, becomes taboo because he is fearful of his feelings. A daughter brought up in this fashion seldom becomes a whole woman. The pathological fear which can do so much damage must be avoided if possible. Good sex education is necessary so that all fathers realize that this kind of feeling is normal."

Edward Brecher agrees with Debbie Anderson that only rarely are incestuous relations between a mother and a son reported to the correctional authorities. "Whether this kind of behavior doesn't happen in real life or whether it means that there are fewer routes by which such incest comes to public attention, I don't know. I don't think anyone knows. Most incest cases involving the father and daughter come to the attention of the authorities when the daughter is thir-

teen to fifteen years old. At some point, the daughter begins
to branch out, and to have boyfriends outside the family.
The father finds difficulty in exercising parental authority
to control the daughter's behavior. At this point she blurts
either to a teacher, a school counselor, or someone else,
who may call the police.

"It may well be that there is no similar machinery of
discovery in the case of the mother-son relationship. Perhaps these cases are genuinely less common in society. I'm
inclined to think they are. They turn up very rarely in therapy literature, for example. Psychiatrists seldom have patients who've had that kind of relationship. It must be a
combination of these factors.

"There are also no accurate figures when the combination
involves siblings. They seem to remain secret with very little
motivation to bring them to light. There is more of a mutu-
ality about it. When parents become aware, they may call
the police, or seek child guidance of some kind, but essentially this does not seem to be a problem for the criminal
justice system. There have been cases where in one family
there was more than one combination of relationships, but
these are oddities. We should not center our attention on
the bizarre situations when considering sex offenses. Warped
thinking about the problem as a whole could result," he
warned.

I came across one such "bizarre" situation during my visit
to a treatment center. I met a husband and wife who were
both guilty of having incestuous relations with the wife's
ten-year-old daughter. The wife had relations with their
two-year-old son as well. Since, as we have seen, compara-
tively few women (between two hundred and three hundred
men to one woman) are sex offenders of any kind, the case
is highly unusual.

At the time I met this couple they were involved in therapy. At present they are outpatients who return to the center
once a week. They willingly talked to me, though the sub-

ject was so full of emotion that on occasion their words
were difficult to follow.

As a child, the wife had been sexually abused by an uncle.
At age sixteen she married for the first time. Her husband
did not believe in birth control, but found her sexually
unattractive when pregnant. Because she gave birth to six
girls in as many years, their sex life was almost nonexistent.
She said her husband would often beat the children, at
times so hard that his hand print was left on their faces. Her
sixth baby died of sudden crib death, and he accused her of
deliberately killing it. During that time, he became enraged
and battered her severely.

Shortly thereafter she met her second husband, who was
at that time still married. His marriage was almost devoid of
sex too. After the birth of his one child during the first year
of marriage, his wife had refused to have sexual relations
again. Both of the couples got divorced; the man and
woman I interviewed lived together until she became pregnant, and then they married.

By then there were six children—her five girls and the one
son of their own. The husband was a butcher and worked
long hours trying to support the large family, while his wife
stayed at home. She said: "I had a lot of pressure on me.
There was no money to hire babysitters so I was at home all
the time. I got no child support from my former husband
and although my present one was always away at work, he
didn't make much money. When I did see him, he paid me
no attention. Our life together was just nil."

In her desperate state of mind she thought that having sex
with her eldest daughter might make her more sexually attractive to her husband. She admitted that she found some
satisfaction in the incestuous relationship, and that her
daughter did not resist her advances at first. Of course, as a
wife she was not more appealing and the home situation
became even more hopeless. "I was on tranquilizers, had
migraine headaches—the kids were sick a lot, and the bills

still piled up." It was then that she made advances to their son. "Yes, my two-year-old son—imagine! I was so messed up, I thought being sexual with him would bring me some relief, but I felt only worse." Several times during the interview she said, "I don't know why I did it to the kids. It was a terrible thing! I really love them—I really do!"

Her husband worked about eighteen hours a day, he told me. "It seemed like it was all the time, but still I couldn't make enough money to pay the bills." He was tired and bored with his whole life. His family situation was so disruptive that coming home gave him no comfort. He felt trapped; the more he worked, the further behind he seemed to get.

One day he read an article in a magazine that suggested a new thrill. "If you're tired of the old lady, try a young girl," it advised. His eldest stepdaughter was the most accessible. Initially, he said, she seemed pleased with the attention, but after three years, it was she who reported her parents. The mother said that she knew what was happening between her husband and daughter, but chose to ignore it.

When they were first formally accused, they pled not guilty, and even fought the case for six months. It took a year of treatment for them to break through their shell of self-hatred and admit that the incest had in fact occurred. The wife said that now, after four years of therapy, she can finally see herself as a person worthy of respect. "What I have done is behind me, and that's where I'm going to keep it."

The daughters all live in foster homes, and she has neither seen nor heard from them since her conviction. If she ever sees them again, the overture will have to be the daughters'. Their son lives with foster parents too, but they are allowed to see him weekends. Within the year, they expect their lives to be stable enough for him to be a part of the family again.

Perhaps this story is more appropriate to the chapter on

treatment, but I include it here because to me these people
are victims as much as are their children—victimized by the
untenable circumstances of their lives. Their irrational solutions were initially difficult for me to believe. How could
anyone think that abusing one's children would solve anything? This is, in my opinion, clearly a case of sexual psychopathy. Normally accepted routes of behavior brought
them only misery. The alternative life seemed to offer un-
tried possibilities for happiness though they really knew
from the onset that their choice was unacceptable. Therefore, admitting to guilt was almost impossible. Analyzed
from this point of view, those who commit sex crimes are
themselves victims as well as offenders.

Germaine Greer discusses statutory rape as another type
of sexual liaison between adults and children. "Sexual intercourse between grown men and little girls is automatically
termed rape under most codes of law. It does not matter
whether the child invites it or even whether she seduces the
adult; he and he only is guilty of a felony. From the child's
point of view, and from the common-sense point of view,
there is an enormous difference between intercourse with a
willing little girl and the forcible penetration of the small
vagina of a terrified child.

"One woman I knew enjoyed sex with an uncle all
through her childhood and never realized that that was anything unusual until she went away to school. What disturbed her then was not what her uncle had done, but the
attitude of her teachers and the school psychologist. They
assumed that she must have been traumatized and disgusted
and therefore in need of very special help. In order to capit-
ulate to their expectations, she began to fake symptoms
that she did not feel. At length, she began to feel guilty
about not having been guilty. She ended up judging herself
harshly for this innate lechery."[1]

Edward Brecher pointed out to me the incest laws in Den-
mark, which consider coercion, not familial relationships,

the more injurious to the children. "The heart of the issue in the law is not that the two persons are different in age or that they are closely related by blood or marriage. The core of it is that one person stands in a position of authority over the other and makes use of this authority to gain sexual access. If a woman is four years older than the age of consent, she can say, 'I want or do not want sexual relations with you.' She can make this decision about anyone who is in a position of authority, and that means a teacher, a doctor, a father, a mother, or an older brother or sister. The crux of the problem then comes into focus— namely, assuming power over another person in the area of sexual relations. These laws are designed to discourage coercive sexual relations with anyone.

"For instance, let us take the situation of a girl of four-teen whose father enters into sexual relations with her. These new laws are exactly like the old ones in that this is a criminal offense. The only difference is that what is singled out as significant is not that this is a father or stepfather but that this is a man in authority over a child. From the age of eighteen on, if that is the age of consent, the law really has no concern over what is consented to; it is simply between the two people. Blood relationship is not the important factor."

Debbie Anderson concurred: "In some societies sexual relations with children and parents or other relatives are accepted. It is considered a practical way of teaching sex—a 'how to do it' lesson. The difference is that the child's needs are considered instead of the parents'. In the United States incest is almost always coercive and that results in tragedy. Our attitude is sexist. We prime males to be constantly sexual and females to be submissive; sexism in all its forms must be eliminated."

# Part Four

# Justice for Whom?

# 9

# Understanding the Judicial Process

Criminal justice as it relates to sex crimes is a contradiction in terms. Too often the courts grant freedom to the rich and imprison the poor. Because people with low incomes cannot afford bail or private attorneys, their chances of being locked up are higher. And in cases of rape, especially in the South, there is a tendency to overpenalize black men for crimes against white women and underpenalize all offenders for crimes against black women.

A prosecuting attorney described how the courts handle cases involving sexual assaults. She explained that county attorneys are responsible for prosecuting all sex offenses that occur within their jurisdictions. They have three priorities: first, to encourage victims to report sex offenses —as we have seen, national estimates show that only a small percentage of sex offenses are reported to the police; second, to minimize the victim's trauma (from the effects of the investigation and prosecution, as well as from the assault itself); and third, to effectively prosecute the case.

After the police have investigated the crime and have identified a possible suspect, the case is brought to an assistant county attorney in the criminal division for its issuance. The prosecutor then contacts the victim for the first time, to acquaint her with the whole procedure. Once the case is found capable of delivery against a particular person, the assistant county attorney decides what accusations will be made. In a sex offense, there is usually a preliminary hearing to determine probable cause. If the need for a trial is established, the victim must testify. Guilty pleas may occur any time up to the beginning of the trial.

Ordinarily the victim's past is not brought up unless the defense is one of consent. If the woman previously has had some kind of voluntary association with the defendant, then the defense will most likely argue that the victim consented to the act. In many states the defense will attempt to cast a shadow upon the victim's character by asking rhetorical questions which could make the jury believe she is not an "innocent" woman. For instance, if she met the man at a party or in a bar and permitted him to take her home, she might be asked: "Isn't it true, Miss So-and-so, that within the last three months you have met six or seven other men in bars, have permitted them to take you home, too, and that you have had sexual intercourse with them as well?" If she denies the accusation the jury may believe that the defense attorney knows something they do not. "No matter what she says, her answer makes it sound like she's hiding something. In such cases, conviction is almost impossible," the prosecutor declared. A judge concurred: "In the last twenty-three cases tried in this court where consent was an issue, the jury found the defendant not guilty." In his opinion, too many jurors use a double standard. They suspect that the women encourage their attackers. One defense attorney remarked that female jurors tend to question the behavior of the complainant even more than do male jurors. He thinks that these women may mentally protect themselves against possible rape by assuming that the victim asked for the attack—something they would never do.

The legal definition of rape varies from state to state, but the main issues generally addressed in all statutes and usually requiring evidence for successful prosecution include lack of consent; actual or threatened force in the commission of the act; and sexual penetration. Medical evidence is crucial, and often focuses on the presence or absence of sperm in the victim. Many accused rapists go free because doctors fail to find semen.

Two Massachusetts researchers recently suggested that perhaps juries should not rely too heavily on the absence of such evidence in reaching their decisions. A study of one hundred and seventy convicted rapists was conducted at the Massachusetts Center on the Diagnosis and Treatment of Sexually Dangerous Persons. The investigators found that a surprisingly large number of men had suffered from sexual dysfunction at the time of rape; almost none reported such difficulty in their nonassaultive sexual relations.

The researchers, A. Nicholas Groth of Harrington Memorial Hospital, Southbridge, Massachusetts, and Ann Wolbert Burgess of Boston College's nursing department, found that 16 percent of the rapists became impotent during their attacks, 3 percent ejaculated prematurely, and 15 percent were unable to ejaculate or had great difficulty doing so. Their conclusion was reinforced by a survey of ninety-two women hospitalized after sexual assaults. No sperm was found in nearly half the patients, including some who had been raped by more than one man.

When the researchers talked with the victims about the sexual dysfunction of their rapists, some were able to report premature ejaculation, retarded ejaculation, or masturbation by the rapist. Many other victims, when asked if the men ejaculated, simply did not know. The inability of victims to recall the sexual dysfunction of their assailants can be attributed to their fear, horror, shock, and desire to forget the experience. Furthermore, although rape is a forced nonconsenting sexual act, many victims may not resist, in order to limit physical trauma. One sees therefore that medical examination may be unduly emphasized in legal proceedings.[1]

Clearly it is difficult to prosecute a sex offender. Another aspect of the trial process that works in the defendant's favor is plea bargaining—pleading guilty to a lesser charge. One county attorney explained the role negotiated pleas play in sex offense cases, and he defended the practice: "Negotiation takes place in almost every case, at least in the beginning. Usually a complaint is made through the police, after which the defendant is given information about the crime he has been accused of committing. We then proceed to gather the necessary evidence needed to prove the case beyond a reasonable doubt. Since the decision of the jury must be unanimous, the defense attorney is required to convince only one juror, while our office must persuade twelve. One juror can create a hung jury and thereby void our prosecution.

"As we go through our case," he explained, "we talk to the witnesses and again to the victim. We want her to know that we're with her, and that we don't doubt her word even though she knows that she will be cross-examined."

But if, as the case proceeds toward the point of picking a jury, a reluctance on the part of the victim or some of the witnesses is sensed, reconsideration is given to having a trial. What once might have been a good case may not be provable by the time of the trial date. If it looks like proof beyond a reasonable doubt is unlikely, negotiation on a reduced charge may begin. It is useless, the attorney believes, to put both the victim and the defendant through the ordeal if it seems impossible for the prosecution to win.

He gave an example: "If a man is charged with burglary or robbery, as well as rape, which is not unusual, we determine the most provable offense. Unless there is a good strong case of rape, the defendant is encouraged to plead guilty to the lesser offense. An attempt is almost always made to negotiate either the length of the sentence or the nature of the charge."

How plea bargaining affects the offender's record was explained: "When the charge is rape and the offender goes to prison for a lesser offense, the original accusation will remain; however, that does not mean he was necessarily guilty of the sexual offense. Because this situation happens so often, there is really no way of knowing how many incarcerated men are sex offenders; therefore, meaningful statistics are difficult to come by. This fact also confuses the rate of repeated sex crimes. An offense that might be termed a first could actually have been committed before."

One judge said he probably would not approve so many cases of plea bargaining if treatment programs were available to sex offenders. He believes that many of his colleagues would also encourage a plea of guilt to the sex crime, thereby giving the offender a chance for treatment referral instead of prison.

This judge's statement gives a clear indication of where the important decisions ultimately lie. Whether it is approval of plea bargaining cases or the sentencing to a long term in prison, it is the judge, rather than the police, prosecutor, or defense attorney who decides the fate of the sex offender.

The principal theme of this book is that we all are more alike than different and that our differences are more a matter of degree than of kind. Sex offenders represent the low end of the social scale; judges represent the high end. However, it is no more true that judges are superhuman than it is true that sex offenders are subhuman. Perhaps, after reading this section, some may feel I overemphasize the power of judges and the potentially devastating results of the misapplication of that power. Few people have experienced a court trial, so it is difficult for them to understand the cruelty a hasty or otherwise ill-considered decision can produce. The judiciary should certainly be respected, but at the same time that respect must be earned and sustained.

From my experience as a court watcher, I am convinced

that changes must be made to check the absolute power of judges. Most of them have orthodox attitudes, have never lived in poverty and, prior to their political appointments, have had little contact with criminals. Even their previous experience in the courtroom is little more than that of the average lawyer. For instance, Marvin Frankel in his book, *Criminal Sentences,* said that before he became a trial judge in 1965, he had spent many years working mainly as an appellate lawyer. He had tried some cases and done a fair amount of trial lawyer's work, but somehow had managed never to face a jury. He had argued criminal appeals, but had never been on either side of a criminal trial. Frankel cites Judge Learned Hand, who was critical of his own sentencing power when he wrote, "Here I am an old man in a long nightgown making muffled noises at people who may be no worse than I am."[2]

In a typical courtroom scene, a judge will read a presentence report, talk to a probation officer, hear pleas for leniency, and will have spent less than an hour in all before pronouncing a sentence of as long as ten years in prison. On one day a judge may feel irritable, and on another affable. Human as these conditions are, a judge's disposition can virtually decide the course of another person's life. There is also conclusive evidence that race and class prejudice, personal views about specific crimes, deformed notions about patriotism, and all sorts of individual quirks affect sentencing.

The problem is that there are few limiting standards, and therefore it is not necessary for judges to state the rationale behind their decisions or even to qualify their opinions. Defendants usually have no choice but to accept the verdict—especially if they are poor.

Judges even differ in sentences imposed on cases presenting similar facts. According to Judge Frankel, "The evidence is conclusive that judges of widely varying attitudes on sentencing, administering statutes that confer huge measures of discretion, mete out widely divergent sentences where the divergences are explainable only by the variations among the judges, not by material differences in the defendants or their crimes. If proof were needed that sentences vary simply because judges vary, there is plenty of it. The evidence grows every time judges gather to discuss specific cases and compare notes on the sentences they would impose upon given defendants. The disparities, if they are no longer astonishing, remain horrible."[3]

Some alternatives to the present system of sentencing have been suggested by its critics—for instance, the use of sentencing councils. These councils would consist of the judge, a psychologist or psychiatrist, a sociologist, and an educator. The main obstacle to their use seems to be the reluctance of judges to invest the added time for considering their colleagues' cases and for attending meetings. Another recommendation is the establishment of training classes for judges. In some jurisdictions, these classes are offered, but they are not mandatory; too often only the best judges attend.

The judicial branch is not the only segment of our criminal justice system that needs reappraisal. The legislative branch, which is responsible for designing and passing our criminal laws, suffers from major weaknesses as well. Norval Morris, in *The Honest Politician's Guide to Crime Control*, notes that, except for the sixteenth century under John Calvin, America has the most moralistic criminal code the world has yet witnessed.[4] In all states criminal law is wide-ranging and especially ineffective in its attempts to regulate sexual relationships and activities.

A sex offense is defined as a violation of any law which prohibits certain types of sexual behavior, as we have seen. In the opinion of Melvin Goldberg, since legislators enact the laws, they, in a narrow sense of the word, make criminals. That which they prohibit becomes improper. Because legislators deal with the law, the normal agency of change is more and more the legislature. Unfortunately, the subject of sex offenses or criminal offenses of any kind is seldom of ongoing interest to elected officials. There are no powerful lobbies of prisoners, jailers, or judges to prod and reward. So legislative action tends to be impulsive—responding to immediate crises, then lapsing into its usual state of inattentiveness. The result is a system of laws which is even more out of date than the way our lawyers, prosecutors, and judges deal with sex offenses.

Many lawyers I talked with felt that we ultimately shall come to admit that society has been mistaken in handing over sex offenders to lawyers and judges. Our present practice is likened to our past custom of entrusting medicine to shamans and astrologers, and surgery to barbers. A hundred years ago we allowed lawyers and judges to have the same control over the mentally ill as they still exert over the criminal groups. It has been pointed out that we now recognize insanity as a highly diversified and complex problem which we entrust to properly trained experts in the field of neurology and psychiatry.

In 1930, Harry Elmer Barnes said: "The diagnosis of the criminal is a highly technical, medical, and sociological problem for which the lawyer is rarely any better fitted than is a real-estate agent or a plumber."[5] However, there seems to be agreement in our society that while psychiatrists and other professionals do have much to contribute, the eventual judgments as to criminal responsibility and the penalties for offenses will continue to lie squarely within the legal order.

# 10

# Punishment or Treatment?

Within the criminal justice system the inhumanity of modern treatment usually is overlooked. Some of the most dehumanizing activities are carried on under the guise of justice and rehabilitation. Our penal system herds society's offenders into locked areas where they continue to perpetrate their offenses on their fellow inmates—men and women who do not have the protection that other citizens have. In the name of control or cure, they are incarcerated, isolated, often shocked and drugged, and their individual rights are violated.

Judge Marvin Frankel observes that very few of us spend much time thinking about criminal justice after there is a conviction, no matter how dramatic or exciting the trial may have been. "Convicts" are the bad guys, and we are the good, so of course they deserve what they get—especially those convicted of sex crimes. Preferring to separate ourselves from such revolting subjects, we tend to draw curtains around them. For the most part, we manage to warehouse our offenders in faraway places, away from their families as well as the rest of us, and then to forget about them.[1]

The intention of criminal justice is to safeguard our lives
and our property. But what is the purpose of prison? Originally prisons in this country were a "humane" response to
capital and corporal punishment. We had learned, for instance, that cutting off the hands of thieves did not stop
people from stealing. It took us a much longer time, however, to learn that killing people for committing rape-murders does not reduce the rate of similar felonies.

Perhaps it is true that prisons do act as a crime deterrent
to those who are potential offenders as well as those who
already are in confinement. But as law professor Melvin
Goldberg has pointed out, most of us are ignorant of the
penalties for different types of crime. While the threat of
imprisonment may prevent some rational vices (such as income tax evasion), in the case of sexual offenses imprisonment is not a very effective deterrent.

Others are of the opinion that the purpose of prisons is to
rehabilitate. But considering the extremely high recidivism
rates (the national estimate is 60 percent), little constructive
rehabilitation seems to be taking place. The truth is that,
with few exceptions, punishment is the sole purpose of
prison. Not deterrence, not rehabilitation, but isolation and
penitence.

Judge Frankel, in *Criminal Sentences,* poses some interesting questions on sentencing: "If the sentence is for punishment, how pleasant should the prison be? If it is for
rehabilitation, is it all right to use the same prison as the one
serving to punish? If we mean both to punish and rehabilitate, is such a thing possible?" Questions like these are
basic, he says, and must be answered. He is amazed at how
many judges have managed to evade them while imposing
millions of years of imprisonment as well as countless death
sentences over the last century or two.[2]

According to Melvin Goldberg, punishment probably is a
necessary product of the criminal justice system; we have a
choice between that or the forming of vigilante justice. If

we were to abolish all punitive aspects of criminal incarceration, the system would break down, say other experts. There has to be some semblance of punishment, they contend. But is the creation of large prisons necessary for this? Massive removal has been the reason for the fortress prisons we maintain, and we the taxpayers are now assessed in excess of twelve thousand dollars per prisoner per year just for lock-ups.[3] Our country cannot afford lengthy removal at this price.

Goldberg has pointed out how deplorable it is that despite statistical evidence indicating that our current prison methods do not work, we are still unable to say: "Look, the possible solution to effective deterrence is a program of rehabilitation." We give this concept much lip service, but we are as yet unwilling to allocate significant money for experimentation and research. This is especially true in the area of sexual crime, even though this kind of offense is the least likely to be deterred by the threat of apprehension and punishment.

Douglas Hall, a defense attorney who operates out of the Legal Rights Center in Minneapolis, Minnesota, also stresses the need for us to consider treatment options. "If the judicial system could adjust to the treatment concept," he said, "and get away from the idea that punishment is the only answer, we could make meaningful improvements in our corrections philosophy." Hall believes that it is essential that sex offenders be treated with sympathy, not revulsion. "The correctional system gives no support to the sex offenders' understanding of their conflicts," he emphasized. He would like to see the procedure changed. "If a man has committed a sex offense, and the nature of the conflict is diagnosed, not having to plead guilty would be much better. Instead, he should be allowed to admit to his participation in the offense by saying, 'I have a problem which causes me to abuse other people, and I want help with it.' I compare his difficulty with that of an alcoholic or a drug addict. In the interest of society as well as the inmates, we simply must make available tools and assistance."

Interviewing judges in various parts of the country produced a variety of pro and con opinions on treatment for sex offenders. One judge, who supports special programs to help sex offenders, said, "Too often, after release, they commit the same crime, and that's no good. We've got to try something different. It may not be the end-all, and it's not going to work for every sex offender, but I'm convinced from my experience that a lot of them could be treated. At present getting help is discriminatory because people with money can go to a private institution for counseling. If the offender proves to the court that he has therapy available, he's more likely to get a suspended sentence. People without money go to prison."

Another judge, who refused to allow the use of my tape recorder during the interview and scowled at my questions, made some rather startling statements. He claimed that psychologists and psychiatrists know little or nothing about offenders in general and sex offenders in particular. In his opinion, only the courts and the correctional system are qualified to make any judgments. (He also stated: "The prison environment creates unlimited opportunities for rapists. They are the ones responsible for most of the sexual assaults in prison.") Evaluating existing treatment programs was difficult for this judge because he was unfamiliar with most of them; however, he had read about Patuxent Institute and spoke well of indeterminate sentencing. The possible danger of extending an inmate's stay longer than necessary did not seriously concern him.

Still another judge had visited a well-established treatment center which is located close to her city. She was favorably impressed with its program, but is disturbed by the attitudes of other judges in her district, who claim that more men escape from the treatment center than from prison, even though they have no personal knowledge of the institution.

"Statistics show that the comparative rates are the same," she claimed. "However, in my opinion, releasing imprisoned men without therapy is similar to escape. They are no better prepared for coping with life on the outside than the escapees. The only difference is the amount of time spent on the inside."

Many people share the belief that treatment programs do not provide adequate security. Robinson Williams, in a lecture presented at the First Annual Conference on the Evaluation and Treatment of Sexual Aggressives, was asked whether the treatment program at Western State Hospital really could protect society from these individuals, yet provide them with a truly supportive and rehabilitative environment at the same time. His reply summed it up well: "Out of 320 men in residence last year, 3 escaped, or 9/10 of 1 percent. This is about one-third the escape rate from correctional institutions in the State of Washington and about as good a record as we are ever likely to achieve in any program for criminal offenders. The cost per day is a little over $20.00, considerably less than for keeping a man in prison in Washington State."[4] As we have seen, Western State is considered to be a highly effective treatment program.

We pour increasing numbers of people into prisons to serve uncertain or indeterminate sentences upon the justification that programs of rehabilitation will be offered to them. But the fact is that in most cases no rehabilitation is available. Few imprisoned sex offenders have access to any kind of individual or group counseling, or even have available any type of therapeutic experience, whether craft therapy or Alcoholics Anonymous. Facing this fact, it is clear that treatment is mostly an illusion.

While it is said that someone must be locked up until he is ready for release, there is no true definition of what "ready" means. And parole boards are especially difficult for the sex offender to deal with because their members have the same prejudices as the average citizen. They are often unaware of available treatment programs, and tend to disregard their possible effectiveness. Sometimes they will allow the offender to go into a program, but too frequently, upon completion, the boards are unwilling to accept recommendations for parole by the treatment centers. The inmate then returns to prison to finish his "time"—the magic cure-all.

The fact is that the majority of prisoners deteriorate in prison rather than improve. They become poorer risks and lesser people. According to William Glasser, this certainly is the case when sentences drag on beyond four or five years.[5] Many sex offenders are included in this group. As one defense attorney said, "Our prisons are feeble. We con the prisoners into thinking that there will be psychiatric help when there is none. We con ourselves into feeling secure, but the lock-up is only temporary. When the prison cage is opened, most of the men go wild. With few exceptions, everyone comes out of the slammer more dangerous than when he went in."

Clearly our judicial system is not geared to the prevention of sex crimes; the average prison sentence is three and a half years, during which time most men become more assaultive. Rather than curing violence, imprisonment can *foster* violent behavior. One prisoner said: "Violence, I feel, is an expression of anger and frustration; an outlet used by those unable to find constructive or legal means by which to voice grievances real or imagined."

Criminal justice agencies such as prisons are seldom crusaders against violence; there is little effort to eliminate the violent peer group subculture that is a part of all penitentiaries. It will take the cooperation of inmate groups themselves to change this system of institutional violence.[6]

A friend of mine who is an incarcerated rapist is using some of his time to study and reflect. He shared these views about the reality of prison life: "I think the idea certainly must have been that the prisoner would have time to reflect on past behavior and so do penitence or repent. With penitentiaries it's still quite evident that penitence is expected. However, that hasn't been the case. The so-called expert penologists have come to realize that since the first prison was built in Pennsylvania by Quakers, punishment simply hasn't worked.

"I don't believe that punishment in and of itself is the answer. It isn't just the perpetrator of the crime who is being punished—there are many other victims. There is the prisoner's family who also suffers, for instance. Not only that, but the suffering prison induces doesn't instill a repentant attitude but rather a bitter one. The environment in this prison is a nineteenth-century one. We are continually reminded in many not-too-subtle ways that we are abnormal, antisocial, and that we do have a very serious behavior problem, for which no help is being offered."

I had met with this offender to discuss a new prison project called Sex Offenders for Treatment. He and his fellow inmates had felt the need to support each other by joining together and sharing their problems. The project's stated purpose was to raise the level of consciousness in the institution by saying, in effect, "We're human beings who need treatment." The program died almost at its inception.

The young man was critical of the unrealistic way in which society deals with criminals, and he concluded our conversation with these words of warning: "For years and years [society] has hidden us behind bars. But the security the public feels is false. I and almost everyone else in this prison will someday get out. The prison may be able to make good inmates out of us, but it will never make us good citizens!"

# Epilogue

It is difficult for many of us to see any human qualities in sex offenders. We feel that we must choose sides—either we are in support of the assaulted victims or we favor trying to find help for the offenders. For me, it is not an either/or, it must be both—both are participants. Unless we try to find out why these ugly acts happen, we have no hope of stopping them. To be interested in a disease (sexual assault) without attempting to find the cause and possible cure is not enough.

We all have the same basic needs for living a productive, self-fulfilling life: (a) the love and respect of ourselves and of other people; (b) a wholesome attitude toward sex; (c) a feeling of responsibility for our own behavior; (d) an understanding of our own potentials and those of others; and (e) a lifestyle that is satisfying to ourselves without being destructive to others.

Sex offenders share these same human needs. They are not born antisocial; their behavior is learned. Extreme sibling rivalry, lack of love from their families, along with great conflict between their parents themselves, are the prime causes of deviancy. Inner rages, frustrations, and a feeling of self-worthlessness result. Sex offenders are lost in the struggle and powerless to change the situation in which they find themselves.

The sad fact is that in our society we often are encouraged to settle our conflicts in violent sexual ways. Movies, books, advertising, and television put a premium on this kind of behavior. We are brought up to believe such sexist myths as: women like to be roughed up; if they say no, they really mean yes; men cannot control their sex drives; women who have poor sex drives enjoy being overpowered. Men are confused by society's image of what is a "real man." The rapist exemplifies the extreme acting out of these attitudes.

We are taught that rape, especially child molestation, is the most heinous of crimes; even murder is more understandable. Although rape is essentially a crime of violence, not sex, assaulted women are usually more damaged psychologically than physically. The way raped women regard themselves sexually, and the support they get from their families and friends affect the extent of their injuries.

Although rape is currently the most feared sex offense, incest and child and wife abuse are equally serious. These practices often are passed on from one generation to the next. As we have seen, the cycle of sexual offense tends to repeat itself.

Since sex offenders, like everyone else, form their habit patterns when they are young, it is important that sex offenses be detected and treated early. Most sex offenders do seem to be susceptible to behavioral changes through therapy, and from my observations, all treatment is superior to just doing time in prison. This opinion is shared by offenders who have experienced both kinds of incarceration.

The most productive and least costly therapy is the self-help therapeutic community approach, with professionals acting as supervisors. The offenders are more apt to express themselves when the groups include only sex offenders.

Having women involved as therapists, and sex education taught as a part of the curriculum, are necessary program components. As we have seen, treated offenders tend to repeat their crimes less frequently than those who are untreated; however, at present there is insufficient money for expanding and properly evaluating the few good programs that are available.

I believe that criminal justice, especially in sex offense cases, is a contradiction in terms; too often only the poor are imprisoned. Judges are considered to be godlike, having few human character and disposition flaws. The truth is that, because of no previous training, most of them are no better qualified to deal with the complexities of a sex offense than the average lawyer. Sharing their decision powers with sentencing councils is one suggested improvement.

As one who has spent much time in courtrooms and prisons, I strongly recommend court watching and prison visitation to all who are interested in personally evaluating our justice system. Getting to know prosecuting and defense attorneys and judges, as well as defendants and victims, is important. Taking a tour of a prison is a good beginning; discussing what you see with an inmate or talking with an inmate group are valuable follow-ups.

There is at present much discussion about the relative merits of indeterminate versus fixed sentencing. The original purpose of indeterminate sentences was to provide incentives for rehabilitation—those who took part in programs might be released earlier. Fixed sentencing, it was rationalized, offered little motivation for reform. As we have seen, inflicting punishment and providing time for penitence are the only purposes of most prisons. Since the object is to punish, not to reform, I believe that eliminating parole boards and fixing relatively short sentences is the most humane approach to incarceration. Sentencing commissions should be established to set guidelines for the judiciary, covering major aspects of sentencing.

It is deplorable that so few treatment centers are available to sex offenders. Most judges are forced to choose between the options of sending an offender to prison, a mental institution or a probation officer. These choices must be expanded; more treatment programs must be provided. Being alarmed at the increase in sex crimes and relieved at the conviction of offenders is not enough. We must determine to change the system.

# Appendices

This section includes in-depth descriptions of two operating sex-offender treatment programs (Appendices A and C); one important experiment that no longer functions (Appendix B); and a summary report outlining a model treatment program for sex offenders in Minnesota (Appendix D), which should serve as an example for other states. Additional material can be obtained by writing to the directors of the nationwide programs listed at the end of the book.

# Appendix A

## The Treatment Program for Sexual Offenders, Western State Hospital, Fort Steilacoom, Washington. (Based on a report by Richard Seely, St. Peter, Minnesota, 1974.)

The 1951 Washington State Legislature, in a piece of legislation referred to as the Sexual Psychopath Law, attempted to establish a truly rational framework for dealing with the habitual sexual offender. The lawmakers were responding to nationwide public alarm at the time over a series of brutal sex crimes. They were convinced that prisons, far from solving the problem, were probably contributing to it. Simple imprisonment seemed to offer nothing constructive; it merely put the offender away for a number of years as punishment for the crime and provided no intensive study of the offender's personality nor treatment for his personality disorder. Imprisonment placed him in an environment utterly unconducive to normality. There was no opportunity for the development of a sense of responsibility in the area of sexual behavior. At the end of his sentence he was released without any representative input by the community in which he had committed offenses.

Implementation of this law by the courts and mental hospitals has gone through three stages during the past twenty years. From 1951-

1957 only a few judges made use of it, and none of the three state mental hospitals developed any specific or effective treatment program for the sexual offender. However, as the numbers of committed sexual offenders increased, pressures grew to develop something specific and appropriate. Western State Hospital, the largest of the three hospitals, began to experiment with self-help programs similar to Alcoholics Anonymous. Also included were group therapy and other behavioral control and modification techniques. This utterly new approach obtained good results, and during the next eight years (1958-66) the techniques constantly were modified and refined. Finally an identifiable, effective treatment model was created. In December, 1966, the program's effectiveness was recognized. It was made available to committed sexual offenders throughout the state. The director of the Washington State Department of Institutions designed the Western State Hospital program. The state's center for the evaluation and treatment of all hospitalized sexual offenders also was located there.

From 1967 on, the small Western State Hospital program entered a phase of rapid expansion and development. In the next four years (1967-70) the annual intake and treatment operation added new treatment services such as work-release, out-patient follow-up and marital counseling. It also provided a regular program of consultation and training for probation officers and others working with the offender in the community. Important research regarding the personality of the sexual offender was begun. The program became in effect a state center, providing a broad range of services.

Once a specialized state center was available, the courts increasingly shifted their commitments to it instead of prison. Where previously the vast majority of these offenders went to prison, during the past two and a half years, the center has received thirty-five percent more than Adult Corrections—one hundred eighty-three to one hundred twenty-two men. During the past year the center has received more than twice as many as Adult Corrections—ninety-four to forty-one men. These figures indicate that essentially conservative courts do make use of a "better mouse trap" when offered one which seems to really work.

Now almost complete cooperation and support have been given by the courts, the Board of Prison Terms and Paroles, and the probation officers. They changed a number of their accustomed procedures to suit the program. With but few exceptions, in the cases of two hundred and eighty-three offenders handled by the center during the past four years, the courts throughout the state have adhered to the program's ninety-day observation recommendations. They have approved a hospital length of stay roughly one-half the time offenders would have had to stay in prison. Support has been given to the program's early work-release and out-patient programs in lieu of protracted institutional residence. Another dividend to the taxpayer is the fact that this particular intensive treatment costs less per day than prison time. This is largely due to the use of offenders as therapists under staff guidance and supervision, rather than a large professional staff to do the treatment.

The program operates on the premise that a specialized state center must maintain close working relationships with the communities from which the offender comes. The center has therefore paid special attention to keeping the judges, prosecutors, and probation officers in these communities informed about developments in their cases and in the program. The center sends out statistical and progress reports at regular intervals. It invites many of these community-based professionals to firsthand observation of therapy operations. Occasional meetings with these personnel are held in their areas of the state. The center has instituted the unusual procedure of having a few probation officers, superior court judges, and jail personnel actually "live-in" on the treatment ward for several days. In this way they get a real understanding of the program's philosophy and treatment methods.

It has taken almost twenty years for the courts to apply the Sexual Psychopath Law in dealing with the majority of the state's committed sexual offenders. The state government has taken just as long a time to develop an effective statewide program. This law's rational approach to the problem has proven to be a wise one. As with all laws, time and hindsight reveal deficiencies, and this law is no exception. For example, the main reason it took so many years to translate legislative intent into program reality was that the law contained a huge gap in practicality. There were no specific provisions for funding, staffing, time-table, or wherewithal to start the new treatment program. Since the hospitals are chronically short of clinical staff, they appointed no one in particular to take responsibility for the sexual offender. No program developed until the offenders posed a critical management problem to the hospitals.

The treatment program is divided into four phases. Phase one involves a ninety-day period of evaluation and observation. The sex offender is assigned to a psychotherapy group and oriented to hospital and group procedures. He completes a biographical data sheet and an autobiography during the first ten days. Then he is given extensive psychological tests and his case is reviewed at an intake meeting. Next, he begins to participate in psychotherapy and other group activities as a trial member. Within ninety days he is evaluated by group and program staffs to determine if (1) he is a "sexual psychopath";* (2) he is "safe to be at large"; (3) he is a good candidate for intensive treatment; (4) he will contribute his share to the self-help program. Then there is a review by the senior staff committee and he is returned to court with the findings and recommendations.

If he is found to be a sexual psychopath and amenable to treatment, he returns for phase two—in-patient treatment. This takes a minimum of twelve months as a general member and group leader. Involvement of wives in psychotherapy and social activities is strongly recommended. Privileges are earned by progress in the four basic treatment objectives: (1) Recognition of his hurtful behavior patterns; (2) Understanding of their origin and operation; (3) Acceptance of responsibility for change; and (4) Application of a new pattern of responsible behavior in dealing with people. Progress on these objectives is expected in all major activities and relationships. (1) Group living; (2) Work assignment; (3) Psychotherapy; (4) Family and sexual

*According to the Sexual Psychopath Law, the term "sexual psychopath" means the existence in any person of the following conditions: (1) Emotional instability; (2) Impulsiveness of behavior; (3) Lack of customary standards of good judgment; (4) Failure to appreciate the consequences of his acts; (5) A combination of any such conditions that render such a person irresponsible for his conduct with respect to sexual matters, and therefore dangerous to other people.

relationship; (5) Social and recreational cooperation; (6) Acceptance of leadership of other members. Privileges are earned by behavior, group vote, and approval by patient and staff leadership.

Requests for discharge as "safe to be at large" on conditional release are under specific conditions of a discharge contract. An examination is required, as well as a vote by the group and a review by the program staff. He is then reviewed by the senior staff committee and returned to court with findings and recommendations.

If the court finds him "safe to be at large," he is placed on probation under specific terms of the conditional release contract recommended by the hospital. He then returns for phase three which is work release. He readmits himself to the hospital for a minimum of three months. There he is employed or attends school in the community forty hours per week. He returns to the hospital at night. He must follow in-patient rules and supervision. His progress is followed by in-patient evening meetings and weekly out-patient meetings. There is a gradual increase in social and overnight leaves as he proves to be responsible.

When proven responsible enough to handle full-time community living, he enters phase four or out-patient treatment. There he attends weekly evening psychotherapy groups for a minimum of eighteen months. Attendance is decreased by request, group vote, and the approval of hospital and parole staff. Continued participation of married couples in psychotherapy groups is strongly recommended.

The program does have some shortcomings, as Richard Seely points out: (1) The education program at the hospital should be improved and should receive a higher priority in the residents' programming. Many of the offenders are undereducated and not trained adequately for any profession. The center should provide more high school, vocational, remedial, and college classes for its residents. (2) Education in the area of human sexuality would greatly enhance the program and help the staff and offenders to deal more adequately with the sexual problems of each individual. (3) More privacy in the wards should be arranged. (4) The law requiring offenders to "pay for" their treatment by receiving no payment for work done needs changing. (5) There should be more involvement with the community on a public relations level. This activity would enhance the relationship with an understanding of the role the community plays in the rehabilitation of the sexual offender.

In spite of these areas that need attention, the program is both humanistic and effective for sexual offenders. To my knowledge, there are none that rank higher. The hospital's small, enthusiastic staff, plus an intensive and well-functioning group of therapists are important components of the program. A well-outlined philosophy and therapeutic approach deal effectively with a large number of sexual offenders in this unique institution.

Approximately eighty percent (two hundred and eighty offenders in 1974) of all of the State's corrected offenders are sent to the Washington State Sex Offender Program by the courts for an evaluation. The recidivism rate for the period 1958 through 1968 was 8.9 percent. None of these persons was re-arrested for crimes more serious than the one he was originally committed for. In comparison, 25 percent of Washington's sex offenders released from prison return within one year of release. Furthermore, of those corrected offenders released since 1968, none have repeated their original offense. Most are employed or attend school full time, and most are relating successfully to adult women.[1]

Appendix B

The Behavioral, Emotional, and Attitudinal Development
Program (BEAD) for Sex Offenders, Minnesota Security
Hospital, 1974–1975. (Based on a booklet by Dr. Ian
Macindoe, Coordinator of the BEAD Program, and Earlyn
Pengelly, St. Peter, Minnesota, 1975.)

## Summary Overview

Although Minnesota law requires that sex offenders be evaluated to
see if treatment is appropriate, no specialized programs have been
available for this purpose since the law was passed more than twenty
years ago. So it has not been possible to require, as a condition of
probation, participation in specialized treatment programs. The great
majority of non-probationed sex offenders have been sent to prison
due to this lack of suitable alternatives, such as a secure facility with
an adequate program for sex offenders. Some sex offenders have been
assigned to the Minnesota Department of Public Welfare for place-
ment in an appropriate state hospital if they appear to have a mental
health disorder which warrants care and treatment in a mental hospital. In most instances these civilly committed sex offenders have been
placed in the Minnesota Security Hospital.

175

In 1974, the Minnesota Security Hospital, with the assistance of the Department of Public Welfare and a grant from the Bush Foundation, established a trial treatment program for a limited period of time with two small groups of sex offenders. The approach adopted was educational in the broad sense. The purpose was to provide experiences in the context of which program participants were encouraged to develop their own behaviors, emotional reactions, and attitudes in ways designed to help them avoid any future anti-social sexual behaviors. For this reason the program was called *Behavioral, Emotional, and Attitudinal Development* (BEAD).

Two groups of men participated in the program. One consisted of fifteen men and the other included fourteen men. They were convicted of sex crimes which involved varying degrees of predatory sexual behavior, from aggravated rape to seduction of children. The first group, BEAD I, was actively involved in the treatment process from May 7, 1974, until October 30, 1974, a total of twenty-six weeks. The BEAD II group was similarly involved from October 1, 1974, until April 23, 1975, a total of thirty weeks. Both groups were involved in program evaluation testing and interviewing for six weeks before participating in treatment and for four weeks after completing the programs.

In outline, the program consisted of approximately fifty hours of sex education, followed by about sixty hours of large group therapy, and varying amounts of small group and individual counseling and therapy. This minimal program was conducted, so far as was possible, to fit in with the regular work and other programs that these men were involved in as full-time residents of the Minnesota Security Hospital (MSH). About half of the work was carried out on Tuesday and Wednesday evenings.

Sex education comprised the first stage of the program. Dr. Bernard Glueck, after completing a three-year study of Sing Sing's sex offenders stated: "The tremendous amount of confusion, distortion, ignorance and anxiety shown by these men—would indicate that there is a need for a much improved program of sexual education—certainly any therapeutic approach to the problems of the sexual offender must have some instruction in sexual matters as an important part of the program."[1] Since this need was obvious with Minnesota's sex offenders also, a thorough sex education was seen as a logical starting point. While classes had been provided for hospital residents a couple of years prior to 1974, the BEAD program provided thorough and comprehensive sex education for sex offenders.

The full-time director of education at MSH held two two-hour sex education classes each week for eight or nine weeks. All fifteen sex offenders participated, along with about an equal number of young women and men from the community. Some of these community participants were teachers or volunteers working in the MSH Department of Education. Five women from the community were co-participants in the BEAD program. These women, recruited on the basis of their maturity, emotional stability, and sensitivity, attended all sex education and large group therapy sessions with the sex offender participants.

The basic purpose of the sex education course was to provide attendants with the opportunity (1) to obtain and discuss accurate sex information under proper educational auspices, and (2) to inquire into and clarify attitudes about a wide variety of human sexual feelings and behaviors. This purpose was achieved with a combination of didactic talks and discussions, the observation and discussion of numerous films, film strips, slides, recordings, and other educational aids. There were also some simple exercises devised to assist participants in comprehending and appreciating their feelings; these exercises were also important to their interpersonal relationships.

Starting with an information-giving approach to sexuality, the course progressed to greater emphasis on understanding and appreciating various behaviors, feelings, and attitudes. The large group would frequently split into small groups of six or seven people to facilitate greater freedom of expression in discussion. Topics dealt with often involved ethical questions, interpersonal affectionate relationships, the distinction between fantasy and action, and the mutual responsibility that sexual partners have toward one another.

The culmination of the sex education course was the special two-day Sexual Attitudes Reassessment (SAR) Seminar conducted by the Program in Human Sexuality at the University of Minnesota.[2] In many respects the SAR seminar resembled the sex education course conducted at MSH. It differed significantly in a number of respects, however. Some of the sex offenders were able to attend with their wives, lovers, or close friends. In addition to the thirty people who had been attending the sex education course there were another forty to fifty people involved in the SAR seminar. The offenders' ability to relate comfortably to these new people during a concentrated two-day program dealing with human sexual behaviors, feelings, and attitudes produced strong responses toward themselves—an extremely important therapeutic catalyst.

The anticipated outcome of all of the sex education described above was an increased degree of psychological comfort for each participant with his own normal sexuality. As well, the experience created a more balanced perspective on his own anti-social behaviors in the past. In the development of a more humane appreciation of the sexuality of others, and the realization that his own sexuality was no different, the sex offender participant's self-esteem was enhanced. He was able to make the distinction between (a) himself as a worthwhile human being and (b) some past behaviors resulting from problems in his life. He was encouraged to think of himself primarily as a person rather than a sex offender.

Large group therapy continued the validation process just described. The large group facilitator (leader), the BEAD program coordinator, and the co-participants met on Tuesday and Wednesday evenings with the BEAD participants. Twenty-two people were too many for much of the work, so the group was split into four smaller groups periodically, with co-participants leading each small group.

The group work tended to deal with the participants' attitudes, present behaviors, and interpersonal relationships. Past difficulties were discussed, considering possible factors in an individual's life which may have contributed, and how similar difficulties in the future could be avoided. The format of each group session varied with the needs of the group. For example, where appropriate the group was presented with problem situations for discussion and/or role playing. When a participant indicated he was ready to work on some of his own problems he would "go on focus"—that is, the group would focus on him and the problems, feelings, attitudes, opinions, and responses he brought out. Considerable probing would often occur in these focus sessions. Although it was understood that nobody was obliged to discuss his past offenses, most men wanted to and did discuss them with the group.

A particular feature which occupied about four large group sessions for both BEAD I and BEAD II was the exchange of tape-recorded group discussions between the BEAD large group at MSH and a group of about four rape victims in Minneapolis. These tape recordings dealt with such topics as: (1) How do I feel personally about my rape experience? What have been my feelings during, immediately after, and long after its occurrence? (2) What experiences did I have to go through because of the rape? How did I feel about my contacts with the police, hospital, attorneys, court, family, friends? (3) Is the act of rape motivated by sexual desire or anger? Is it mainly sexual or aggressive? (4) Is rape an act against the victim, or against women generally, or against society, or what? What causes or motivates a man to rape? After listening to the victims discussing these topics the BEAD group gave their own ideas on the subject. These were recorded and listened to by the victims in Minneapolis. The victims talked about what they had heard; it was taped and then played for the BEAD participants whose subsequent discussion was taped, and so on.

The purpose behind this exchange of rape tapes was to try to provide the offender participants with an empathy-inducing perspective on rape from the victims' point-of-view. Sex offenders have been described as having in common ". . . a serious defect in interpersonal relationships, an absence of mature, selfless concern for the victim. . . and a totally narcissistic, self-center orientation."[3] The aim of the exchange of tapes with rape victims, and the aim of the BEAD program generally, was to help the participants develop a less self-centered, a more concerned, and a more mature feeling toward other people.

Small groups and individual counseling were more readily available to the BEAD II group than to the BEAD I group. In September, 1974, four graduate students at Mankato State College were hired to spend 12 hours per week as counselor-therapists with the BEAD II participants. They also carried out one-to-one work with the six BEAD I men who were most in need of continuing help after the formal termination of the BEAD I program in November. (The BEAD program coordinator had conducted two small groups in lieu of individualized work with BEAD I participants. His other responsibilities prevented him from carrying out the individual counseling and therapy that was needed. As it became clear that the program was understaffed these part-time staffing arrangements were made to correct the situation for the second BEAD group.) The counselor-therapist conducted small groups and individualized sessions with their clients regularly during the first four months of 1975.

Evaluation of the program was designed to determine whether the program was effective and worthwhile. The twenty-nine sex offender participants of the program were compared with matched controls at the Minnesota State Prison. The prison control sex offenders were matched primarily for type of offense, then in terms of intellect and education, age, and socio-economic status (as measured by vocational background). Fifteen prisoner controls were matched with the fifteen participants in BEAD I. Unfortunately, six months later only six prisoners volunteered as controls matched with the men in BEAD II. (The other imprisoned sex offenders were angry at not receiving treatment themselves and expressed their frustration by refusing to act as control subjects.)

In the long run the criterion against which the test and interview data must be evaluated is the number of men from each group, either BEAD participants or prisoner controls, who are arrested, charged, and convicted of a new sex felony. Such data should be collected annually over the next decade. In the meantime the participants and the controls can be compared in terms of pre-program to post-program changes in their test and interview scores. These data derive from (a) goal attainment scaling to measure the degree to which the men achieve goals to strive for over the period of the program; (b) tests of sexual knowledge and sexual attitudes, and some related tests; (c) measures of moral maturity level; (d) content analysis of the rape tapes; and (e) a variety of other psychometric tests. It was hypothesized that the BEAD participants would produce greater overall score changes than would the prisoner controls.

The small number of sex offenders involved necessarily precluded any sophisticated statistical treatment of the data, and the results must be construed as suggestive only. The evaluation aspect of the experimental phase of the BEAD program is of most value in providing experience and guides for future work.

Problems and shortcomings are to be expected in initiating programs of this type. According to Ian Macindoe, the experimental phase of the BEAD program had its share of them. Perhaps the major shortcoming was the "thinness" of the program. Men participating in the experiment spent between four and seven hours per week receiving BEAD treatment—an extremely brief time when spread over six months. The program could have been spread over twelve months, but only fifteen men instead of twenty-nine would have received help. A better alternative would have been a more intensive program involving, say, six therapeutic hours per day. This would require more staff and some internal reorganization within the hospital. Of course, ideally there should be a semi-autonomous twenty-four hour program with its own staff; but this would be an entirely different program.

Another shortcoming was the inability to deliver the kind of treatment that some of the participants needed. This included aversive-styled work for a few men whose problems were appropriate for this kind of help. A great deal more could have been done in the area of co-marital counseling if staff and facilities had been available.

A few of the more obvious problems can be touched upon briefly. Because the initial phase of the BEAD program was experimental, involving pre- and post-program data collection, and because it was not known whether the program could continue beyond June, 1975, it was not open-ended. That is, all participants in BEAD I began and ended their treatment at the same time. The same was true for BEAD II. This meant (a) men who needed additional help beyond the end of the program were left without it (although, in practice, this problem was largely overcome) and (b) men who entered the hospital after the start of the program could not be included for treatment (again, in practice, this was true only in the sense that they had to wait until the next group of participants was formed).

The transfer of sex offenders from the prison to MSH for participation in BEAD also created some difficulties. It wasn't possible for the

BEAD coordinator or the MSH staff to screen potential participants in the Minnesota State Prison or the State Reformatory. These men were selected by the clinical psychologists at those institutions and, while they were very appropriate for treatment from the BEAD staff's point of view, they were not typical of the hospital residents with whom the MSH staff was accustomed to working. There was a general feeling that they presented a management problem within the hospital. This situation not only provoked a great deal of disharmony within the hospital staff, but it placed the BEAD program in the role of an irritant to the smooth running of the institution. Even more importantly, the uncertainty of their post-program disposition produced in the BEAD participants motivational blocks which seriously impaired their therapeutic work.

*Intensive Treatment Program for Sexual Aggressives*
## Guidelines for Unit Living
As Described by the Sex Offender Residents

1. The overall purpose is to create a living situation that allows the individuals of the unit to learn and develop so that they can return to the community as useful and productive individuals.

2. *All individuals of the unit are expected to act in a socially acceptable manner at all times.*

  a. Everyone is awakened at 7:00 a.m. There is no lying down between the hours of 7:00 a.m. and 9:00 p.m., except by special permission. There is no set time for going to bed or for turning off the television.

  b. No more than $35.00 per person is allowed on the unit at any one time. This is for security reasons.

  c. No relationships are permitted which reinforce irresponsible patterns of social-sexual behaviors.

  d. No selling, trading of expensive goods or valuables are allowed without the permission of small group or unit.

  e. Ward clean-up is expected of everybody on the unit. Jobs are done daily before the members leave the unit.

  f. All small group and unit meetings hold precedence over visits, work, or any other interests, excluding testing.

  g. Cafeteria rules must be followed.

    1. Wait until unit is called for meal and all residents who are working return to unit prior to going to meal.

    2. There are no restroom breaks after line-up is called or while in cafeteria. Only by special permission is one allowed to leave.

    3. Before going back for seconds all wards must be fed.

    4. All residents must eat in designated areas for their unit.

## Individual Responsibilities to the Community

1. We must admit that we have behavioral problems. These problems have caused us to act irrationally and to become dangerous to others and ourselves.

2. We must make commitments to correct our behavioral problems.

3. We must take an inventory of our lives by looking at ourselves, our attitudes, our thoughts, and our relationships with ourselves and other people.

4. We have to admit to ourselves and others the exact nature of our irresponsible actions.

5. Through practice, knowledge, and self-discipline we will learn to be compassionate, thoughtful, and in-touch with our own and others' feelings.

6. We must accept all rules and regulations. They are:

  a. We must not abuse, antagonize, or in any way threaten ourselves or others.

  b. Physical violence in no way is tolerated on or off the unit.

  c. We must respect other people and their property.

  d. Attending all unit functions and meetings is required.

  e. Residents may sleep from 9:00 p.m. to 7:00 a.m. Monday through Friday; on Saturdays and Sundays and holidays from 9:00 p.m. to 9:00 a.m.

  g. All beds are made and each area kept clean.

  h. No sleeping during the day is allowed. (Sick pass excluded.)

  i. Two members will accompany sick person to nurse's station to verify sickness.

j. All questions and problems should be taken up with assigned "Big Brother" or small group.

k. Chairman of council will audit ward treasury once a month.

# The Big Brother Support System

This system is designed for the individual who has just become a member of the community, and for those in the community who need special help. It is also to assist individuals of the community in developing and in becoming a part of the community. Big Brothers are assigned for an indefinite period of time. Any responsible member of the community, who has been on the unit at least 60 days, can be a Big Brother.

The Big Brother is responsible to the unit for:

1. The actions of the individual.

2. For getting to know the new resident, and reporting his progress to the group weekly.

3. Being available whenever the individual needs him to talk to or to answer questions.

4. Acting as an escort whenever needed.

The small group will assign a Big Brother when it is felt that the resident is not:

1. Abiding by the rules and regulations of the community.

2. Taking an active part in the community.

3. Showing responsibility to both the community and himself. Every new member of the unit who is involved in the evaluation process is assigned a Big Brother.

A community member no longer needs a Big Brother only when he:

1. Knows the community rules and regulations.

2. Is taking an active part in the community.

3. Has shown responsibility to both the community and himself for his actions.

4. Feels that he no longer needs a Big Brother.

# Small Group Therapy Sessions

Everyone in small group is here for a sexual offense, which is irresponsible behavior. Since all behavior is learned, somewhere along the line, our treatment process provides a medium for us to re-learn responsible behavior patterns so that we can again become productive and beneficial members of society.

It is through small group that we re-learn ways to control such emotions as anger, hostility, depression, frustration, and jealousy. We also learn how to be assertive in our behaviors instead of being aggressive, as most of us have been in the past. We also learn to be loving, caring, understanding, and empathetic instead of apathetic.

The main purpose of small group is to provide therapeutic counselling for the participants, all of whom have emotional and behavioral problems. The process idea is for the group to focus on an individual member's problem. It also offers suggestions as to ways of changing the behaviors which reinforced the problems.

Small group is designed for a maximum of ten members with two group supervisors, one male and one female, whose purpose is to guide and teach. During a focusing situation, the group works together in a constructive manner. It points out and offers helpful suggestions as to changing attitudes which are contrary to responsible social/sexual behavior.

The group decides as a whole whether or not a member is living up to his commitments; they decide on any change in security or authorization for a pass. Small group also decides if a person should be escorted on his visits. When voting on issues in group, members must vote either "yes" or "no." Abstentions are not acceptable.

Each member of Small Group has many responsibilities to himself and his group. These are as follows:

1. Each member is expected to attend all small group meetings and to be prompt.
2. Each member is required to prepare and present to group his autobiography. This sketch should be honest and should include all feelings and experiences that can be recalled from the beginning of your life.
3. Each member is required to write commitments to himself, small group, and the program in the form of short-term goals.
4. Each member is expected to be actively involved, to learn, and be concerned about the other members' progress.
5. Everyone should give moral support to members during rough

periods. Suggestions should be given as how to deal with problems of emotion, behavior, stress, and confusion.

6. Each member is expected to do weekend caring exercises, chart-
ing, and any other assignments which may be given them, by
either group or staff.

7. Each member is to ask for help on problems whenever he has
them. Small group does not end when the two-hour session is
over; it's a twenty-four-hour-per-day process. Members are to talk
with others in an effort to understand them better, to help them
with problems, negative attitudes, and lonely feelings. Members
are expected to show each other the true meaning of care and
concern, through our actions as well as our words.

8. Members are expected to confront others on any and all inappropriate behaviors, to talk about them and offer constructive criti-
cisms and ways to positive change. If necessary, their problems
should be brought to small group.

Small group therapy is treatment, not punishment. If it is looked at
in this manner the benefits become much easier to obtain. Nothing
that is worth having is easy to get. This program is not easy; it is hard.
There are many unpleasant feelings involved in changing one's behavior and attitudes pattern. The program will work only if you want it
to. By being open in small group you won't have to do it alone. Above
all, small group is not a threat to your existence. It is a tool to be used
to better understand yourself as others see you. It is held for two
hours a day, eight hours a week.

## Large Group Therapy Sessions

We meet three times weekly with staff as a large group. On Wednes-
days at 1:00 P.M. all the staff and residents meet together for one
hour, and on Tuesdays and Thursdays at 2:30 P.M. we meet to study
sex education.

Wednesday's large group is designed as a tool for residents to better
their communication with staff and vice versa. It is here where we
discuss problems we are having on the unit, the treatment philosophy
and any problems we may be having with treatment. On Tuesdays and

Thursdays we have sex education. Some of the things we are re-learning are:

1. The difference between the myths and the facts inherent in human sexual practices.
2. How to have loving, caring relationships without sexual inter-course.
3. That women are equal to men and not mere objects for our sexual wants.
4. To accept other life styles that are different from our own, i.e., homosexuality, bisexuality.
5. The senseless stereotypes that surround most of these beliefs.
6. That most sexual fantasies are healthy.
7. How to change a fantasy that could serve as a reinforcement for an inappropriate sexual and/or social behavior.

Through this relearning process we are able to better understand our own misconceptions about human sexuality and come in contact with the areas of our own personal makeup which require change.

## Appendix C

**Intensive Treatment Program for Sexual Aggressives Minnesota Security Hospital Guidelines For The Therapeutic Community. (From a report by Richard Seely, Director of I.T.P.S.A., St. Peter, Minnesota, 1977.)**

The Sex-Offender Treatment Program at Minnesota Security Hospital is asked to perform three tasks: 1) to make those in the Sex Offender Unit understand that society will not tolerate certain destructive or irresponsible sexual behaviors; 2) to protect society, for temporary periods of time, from those persons whose previous aggressive acts were socially dangerous; and 3) to prepare those persons to be responsible members of society when they are released from the program.

The Intensive Treatment Program for Sexual Aggressives team has chosen to create a therapeutic community. Its treatment has three primary models: 1) the custody model, 2) the medical model and 3) the social model. These three disciplines are often in conflict with one another yet each has a valuable contribution to make to any comprehensive treatment program.

*The custody model* is often referred to as the correctional model. It brings to a sexual offender treatment program security, protection of potential victims, and enough time to effectively change behavioral patterns which are not socially acceptable.

*The medical model* provides necessary intervention for those individuals whose psychiatric diagnosis includes various categories of mental illness or overt psychosis.

*The social model* provides the necessary reinforcers to change attitudes, behaviors, and emotional control. It also supplies twenty-four-hour-per-day observation of the offenders' interaction with others. The treatment team attempts to create the conditions under which a sexual offender can begin to act as a responsible member of a community.

This choice of direction reflects the following assumptions:

1. These three basic models unite to effectively deal with the task of helping an offender understand his basic problems by learning to change his behavior, his attitudes, and the way he copes with his environment.

2. Sexual offenders are basically like other people in their desire to be respected and to have close, growth-producing relationships. However, their inability to delay immediate gratification allows them to behave in socially unacceptable ways. Under therapeutic conditions that support more desirable attitudes, most offenders show some capacity to change.

3. Sexual offenders who have the opportunity to act as responsible community members while in the hospital should be able to deal more effectively with the expectations of society. Participation in the I.T.P.S.A. treatment process, which encourages social responsibility, will at least help the offender to behave more responsibly; and at best, will increase his ability to act consistently in an accountable manner.

4. Most sexual offenders view the sequence of the offense, the arrest, the evaluation and commitment or sentencing as major disruptive crises in their lives. Like most people in crisis, they need the assistance of others to make necessary constructive adaptations ranging from human support to complicated therapies.

5. Sexual offenders utilize the help from others only as they

perceive it in their own immediate reality. Through the treatment
process they do the work of preparing themselves for the return to
society. The team and peers can only encourage and influence the
direction of learning, personal growth and change.

6. The sexual offender tends to be especially naive about sexuality
and its relationship to his personal life. He often seems to integrate it
into his self-concept and his expressions of rage, hurt, anger, and frustration. Often the result of this integration is the victimization of
another person.

7. By dehumanizing others, sex offenders justify their irresponsible
sexual behavior. Their attitudes are sexist. They rarely have a positive,
growth-producing relationship with another person, especially with a
woman. Sex offenders tend to be "loners" and many have histories
of chemical abuse.

8. The ITPSA's treatment process involves the "therapeutic
community" which confronts positive and negative behaviors from a
reality oriented perspective. The offender has violated basic human
rights in our society. Previously the courts punished the offender by
isolating him from the community. Minnesota Security Hospital is
staffed primarily by attendant guards whose first responsibility is
to provide custody and security to the institution. The program's
ultimate responsibility is to retain the offender under custody until
he has been determined to be "safe-to-be-at-large" in the open
community.

9. Human rights are basic to acquiring social skills in group living.
A good human relationship must include individual dignity, respect
and concern for the rights and welfare of others, and reliance on
positive social controls.

10. ITPSA chose the therapeutic community as the model for
developing growth-producing relationships with fellow residents,
staff and volunteers. There, social mores can develop, encouraging
the values and mores of society as a whole. The therapeutic community
then becomes a social unit capable of generating and shaping appropriate socializing processes. Each person thus becomes a "member of
a group."

# Psychological Measurements of Intensive Treatment Program for Sexual Aggressives

*The Minnesota Multiphasic Personality Inventory:* This measurement is designed to provide an objective assessment of some of the major personality characteristics that affect personal and social adjustment. The carefully constructed and cross-validated scales provide a means for measuring the personality status of residents together with a basis for evaluating the acceptability and dependability of each test record.

*The California Psychological Inventory:* This measurement is concerned with characteristics of personality which have a wide and pervasive applicability to human behavior, and which in addition are related to the favorable and positive aspects of personality rather than to the morbid and pathological. Its scales are addressed to personality characteristics important for social living and social interaction, i.e., to variables that are woven into the fabric of everyday life. "Folk concepts" such as these appear to be relevant to the prediction and understanding of interpersonal behavior in any setting, culture, or circumstance.

*The Adjective Check List:* This measurement offers words and ideas commonly used for description in everyday life in a format which is systematic and standardized. This enables an individual to describe himself from his own perspective. In addition to providing information on counseling readiness, diagnosis, and prognosis for therapy, the Adjective Check List gives an objective indication of individual self-concept and self-esteem.

*Wechsler Adult Intelligence Scale:* This instrument measures verbal and performance ability over a wide range of areas. The subscales provide data regarding learning problems, potential ability, attention span, reasoning, auditory and visual imagery, visual perception, visual-motor integration, analysis of relationships, language development, recall, concept formation, and organization of knowledge.

*The Sex Inventory:* This measurement was developed for use with sex offenders. The items sample a wide range of sexual behaviors and provides information about sex interests, drives, attitudes, adjustment, conflict, cathexes, controls, and sociopathic tendencies.

*The Bender-Gestalt Test:* This measurement is used to detect damage to the cortical areas of the brain.

# Intensive Treatment Program for Sexual Aggressives Group Involvement Scale Criteria for Evaluation of Small Group Participation

| 1 | 2 | 3 | 4 | 5 | 6 | 7 | 8 | 9 |
|---|---|---|---|---|---|---|---|---|
| No Involvement | | | | Average Involvement | | | | Excellent Involvement |

| Score | Criteria |
|---|---|
| 0 | Absent |
| 1 | Person is present in group session. Person sits in group and does not say anything. Person does not appear to be actively taking notes or writing questions. When questioned, person offers only non-informative answers. |
| 2 | Person makes one or two pertinent comments or asks one or two pertinent questions. Person seems to be attempting to entertain, tell "war stories," and/or con group. Person's involvement does not seem sincere. Confrontations seem revengeful and selfish. |
| 3 | Person appears to be awake, attentive, and seems to be involved in the topic under discussion. Person makes one to three pertinent comments and asks one to three pertinent questions. |
| 4 | Person seems to be really attentive, actively listening, and asks four to six pertinent questions or makes four to six personal comments during the group. Person relates what is being said to a personal experience or feelings at least once during the group. |
| 5 | (Average Involvement) Person appears to be really attentive, actively listening, and involved. Person relates what is being said to personal experience or feelings two or three times during the |

group. Person makes six or more pertinent comments or asks six or more pertinent questions. Person provides some new information about himself to the group. Person does not appear to be attempting to entertain, tell "war stories," and/or con the group. Person's verbal and non-verbal behavior appear to support each other.

6   Person relates what is being said to a personal experience or feelings at least four times during the group. He relates self to other's problems without attempting to change the focus and takes an active responsible role in keeping the group moving in the focused direction.

7   Person offers information about himself and some degree of insight as to what has changed. Person appears to have some understanding about what his behavior has meant to other people and expresses empathy with either other residents or victims.

8   Person expresses empathy and serious concern for the rights of others. Person appears to be open and straight-forward in his comments, seems to have a good understanding of himself, and expresses this in group.

9   Person is consistently involved and is consistently frank in his comments. Person's involvement continues throughout the group and his verbal and non-verbal behavior consistently support each other. Person gives a considerable amount of insight into the focused material.

## Intensive Treatment Program for Sexual Aggressives Phases and Steps of Progress

The first thirty to ninety days the offender goes through an evaluation phase. Within that time he must be judged by the group and team not to be an escape risk. Phase One is called In-Patient Treatment and each step requires a minimum of thirty days for completion. Here the candidate must prove to the group that he has a basic understanding of group words, on- and off-ward policies, and regulations of group expectations for responsible behavior. He must also understand why he chose his outlet (deviant behavior) and must score an average of 2.0 on the Group Involvement Scale. (See Scale on pp. 192–93.)

In Step Two, he learns and understands his hurtful behavior as demonstrated by progress in the modification of those behaviors. He must understand the program philosophy, and scores an average of 2.5 on the Group Involvement Scale over the previous month.

He learns in Step Three his basic problems and applies techniques he has learned from reading and group interaction, to change behavior and habits. He is also involved and shows concern for others in unit activities, and must average 3.0 on his G.I.S., over the past month.

During the next step (Four) he gains knowledge of program values and how they are applied to behaviors and feelings. He knows more about his fantasy and behavioral outlet patterns and applies these "stop signs" to controls, feelings, fantasies, and desires. He averages over the previous month 3.5 on his G.I.S. score.

Step Five aids him in adopting a help-seeking attitude, in controlling fantasies and desires, and building consistent responsible behavior in interpersonal relationships. A 4.0 average G.I.S. over the previous month is required. By the time he finishes Step Six, he must display knowledge of early deviant behavior patterns, and how these patterns developed to current behavior. As well, he demonstrates further progress in control of fantasies. His G.I.S. must average 4.5 over the past month.

The offender must set during Step Seven a good example to other group members in the application of responsibility; he understands the concepts of dehumanization and how it affects relationships. His G.I.S. average must be 5.0 over the previous month. Achieving the ability to apply therapeutic methods and to guide the group is accomplished in Step Eight. The offender must show that his new outlets are under control and that he is consistantly responsible. 5.5 over the past month is his G.I.S. average.

He becomes effective in handling leadership responsibility with the staff, program members, and outside contacts in the ninth step. In all of his relationships, he reacts out of concern and responsibility, and he averages 6.0 on his G.I.S. over the past month.

Phase Two, Step Eleven covers a period of two months during which time he must show added responsibility, care, and concern for others even though he has no leadership responsibilities. Phase Three, Step Twelve requires three months. The resident now is in full control of his behavior, and his outlets are realistic and logical (no longer deviant).

Three months are required to complete Phase Four, Step Thirteen. The group and staff are now comfortable with the resident's ability, honesty, and effort in his day-to-day functioning. The next three months, in Phase Five, Step Fourteen, the man continues to be involved in mature, nondeviant, nonexploitive, nonmanipulative, and nonpredatory attitudes. When he completes the last phase and step (Six and Fifteen), which requires a minimum of twelve months, all of his behaviors, work, and psychological reports are consistently favorable. His relationships are clearly growth producing, and a support system is firmly established.

Although the total program takes a minimum of five years and one month for completion, during the last year and nine months, the resident is gradually released to the community. When he reaches Phase Three, Step Twelve, he is eligible for work and/or school off-campus up to eight hours per day. He can visit with his family or a significant other for one weekend per month. Leaving the hospital five days and nights per week, and returning weekends, is allowed during Phase Four, Step Thirteen.

In Phase Five, Step Fourteen, he may leave the hospital but must return for one weekend per month beginning on Friday evenings. He is released from the hospital in Phase Six, but during the year, he is required to contact the therapist supervisor and, once a month, to take a psychological test battery during one visit to the hospital within each six-month period. He also sends any written reports as requested, and his support system is examined and approved by the I.T.P.S.A. team. Since this program has been in existence such a short period of time, as yet no offenders have been released. As Edward Brecher said, it seems to have all the components for effective therapy, and so he expects it to be successful as a treatment center.

## Appendix D

Sex Offenders and Their Treatment in Minnesota
A Summary Report of the Project to Design and Develop
an Organizational and Rehabilitational Model for the
Treatment of Sex Offenders in Minnesota.

A common weakness in the organization of sex-offender treatment programs is a lack of statewide coordination. Minnesota is no exception. Each treatment center runs independently, raising its own finances, and administering its own therapy. The following is an excerpt from the Minnesota report which was conducted to develop a model for a statewide treatment plan.* The full text of this report may be obtained by contacting Dr. Lance Wilson, Correctional Service of Minnesota, 1427 Washington Avenue So., Minneapolis, Minnesota 55454. It is hoped that this plan can serve as a model for other states.

There are six specific recommendations in the report. The current fragmentation of treatment services and minimal information coordination between state departments, counties, and others dealing with sex offenders may be lessened over the next few years by a clear

*Dr. Thomas Correll, an anthropology professor at Bethel College in St. Paul, Minnesota, conducted and collected the research for this model.

196

definition of responsibility. Thus, the first recommendation is that:

1. The Minnesota State Department of Corrections provide the mechanism for increased communication and coordination between the agencies which now have responsibility for sex offender assessment, treatment, outreach, and evaluation;

There is no program in the prison or reformatory specifically designed for the treatment of sex offenders. Thus, the second recommendation is to:

2. Develop and implement a Pilot Program for the Treatment of Sex Offenders in the Prison/Reformatory;

During the course of the research it became clear that there is little communication and information exchange between treatment professionals in the various community, institutional, and private sex-offender treatment settings in Minnesota. It is thus the third recommendation of this project to:

3. Develop and implement a forum for information exchange among sex-offender treatment professionals in Minnesota; The fourth recommendation is:

4. Improve data collection and coordination concerning sex offenders in state hospitals, in prison/reformatory, and on probation and parole;

There are 43 identified community-based treatment programs in Minnesota that provide treatment to sex offenders. The fifth recommendation is to:

5. Conduct a systematic evaluation of the effectiveness of Minnesota community-based treatment programs which treat sex offenders;

Throughout the research several unanswered questions arose concerning the nature of sex offenders and the causes and correlates of their behavior. The search of relevant literature provided little guidance. The final recommendation is to:

6. Encourage research efforts to study the nature of sex offenders and the causes and correlates of sex offensive behavior.

The better understanding of reasons for sex-offender behavior may lead to better treatment modalities. A general model for a continuum of treatment services for the sex offender was developed. The continuum is designed to serve the offender through three stages: assessment, treatment, and outreach. The model is sufficiently general to be used as a guide in developing specific community and institutional programs.

The treatment system model proceeds on the assumption of a need for both systematic eclecticism and holism: eclecticism because no single treatment modality has emerged with an "always effective" solution, and holism because offenders are viewed as complex multi-faceted interacting systems.

Assessment is a process of determining an offender's need for, interest in, amenability to and potential performance in treatment. Assessment procedures include, but are not limited to, the following techniques: observation, interview, medical examination, psychological testing, behavioral measurement, review of prior records and reports. The outcome of an assessment should be a recommendation or plan for the treatment (or recommendation for no treatment) of the offender.

Treatment specifies a set of therapeutic operations and conditions which the offender requires and experiences as part of a planned program for his rehabilitation. Specific treatment programs are suggested to contain at least an emphasis upon the following elements: goals; phases; therapeutic community; social systems; sexual health and education; and living skills.

Outreach is a category of services that are available to the graduates of a treatment program in the form of follow-up or aftercare, and to others who may wish to receive treatment for a related problem on the basis of self-referral. Outreach may include a variety of services to the offender among the following: preparation for release and the creation of post-release guidelines, aftercare, satellite programs, and the creation and continuance of community support groups.

Taken together, these three kinds of service constitute an over-lapping continuum. Knowledge gained by means of assessment becomes the basis for a treatment plan. Treatment follows the plan in terms of a set of specific therapeutic goals. Outreach is basically delivered to the offender in terms of guidelines consistent with the therapeutic experience.

Evaluation is suggested as an important adjunct component of the model. A three-level approach to evaluation is suggested to provide outcome, process, and comparison measures. It is important to foster and continue an administrative and professional staff commitment to the evaluation process. Specific evaluation designs can only be created in response to specific treatment programs.

Finally, an adjunct training component is suggested to provide information concerning sex offenders and their treatment; problems and prospects of various theoretical and applied approaches to assessment, treatment, and outreach; and the logic, problems, implementation, and utilization of program evaluation. Specific training methods may include the following: symposia, colloquia, workshops, and seminars. The target population for training is those persons involved with the treatment of sex offenders in Minnesota.

The model provides a general structure within which specific assessment procedures, treatment modalities, and outreach services can be designed, operationalized, and evaluated. Until it is possible to isolate the causes of antisocial sexual behavior and develop methods to successfully treat the offenders, it is advised to proceed in a cautious, experimental, open-minded and well-evaluated manner. This model provides a structure for this proceeding.

# Directors of Nationwide Treatment Programs for Sex Offenders

**California**

Dr. Henry Giarretto, Director
Child Sexual Abuse Treatment Program
Juvenile Probation Department
County of Santa Clara
840 Guadalupe Parkway
San Jose, California 95110

Alfred J. Rucci, M.D., Medical Director
Atascadero State Hospital
Drawer A
Atascadero, California 93422

Richard and Rosemary Bryan
SOANON (Sex Offenders Anonymous)
P.O. Box 8287
Van Nuys, California 91409

Seymour Pollack, M.D., Director
Program for Sex Offenders
Institute of Psychiatry, Law and Behavioral
    Sciences

Los Angeles County/University of Southern
   California Medical Center
Room 132
1237 No. Mission Road
Los Angeles, California 90033

Dr. Frank Vanasek
Program for Sex Offenders
Patton State Hospital
Patton, California 92369

**Colorado**          Dr. Nancy M. Steele
Treatment Program for Sex Offenders
Colorado State Reformatory
Box R
Buena Vista, Colorado 81211

**Florida**           Dr. Geri Boozer
Treatment Program for Sex Offenders
South Florida State Hospital
1000 S.W. 84th Avenue
Hollywood, Florida 33023

Benjamin Ogburn, M.D., Director
Sex Offender Program
Forensic Unit
Florida State Hospital
Chattahoochie, Florida 32324

**Maryland**          Martin Katzenstein, Director
Sex Offender Treatment Program
Baltimore City Jail
Eager Street
Baltimore, Maryland 21202

Jonas R. Rappaport, M.D., Project Director
Outpatient Treatment Clinic for Special Offenders
Institute of Psychiatry and Human Behavior
University of Maryland
645 West Redwood Street
Baltimore, Maryland 21201

Michael Spodak, M.D.
Ann Falck, R.N.
Office of Psychohormonal Research
Phipps Clinic
The Johns Hopkins Hospital
Baltimore, Maryland 21205

**Massachusetts**     Richard J. Boucher, Director
Massachusetts Center for the Diagnosis and
   Treatment of Sexually Dangerous Persons
Box 554
Bridgewater, Massachusetts 02324

**Minnesota**     Richard Seely, Director
Intensive Treatment for Sexual Aggressives
Minnesota Security Hospital
St. Peter, Minnesota 56082

Jim Martinson, Director
Alpha House
2712 Fremont Ave. So.
Minneapolis, Minnesota 55408

William W. Duffy, Executive Director
Center for Behavior Therapy, Inc.
606 24th Ave. So.
Minneapolis, Minnesota 55454

**New Jersey**     William Prendergast, Director of Professional
   Services
Adult Diagnostic and Treatment Center
Lock Bag R
Avenel, New Jersey 07001

Frederick Rotgers, Director of Psychology
Treatment Program for Sex Offenders
State Prison
Trenton, New Jersey 08625

**New Mexico**     Ms. Judy Fleischman
Ms. Margot Berger
Counsellors-in-charge

Treatment Programs for Sex Offenders
Alternatives, Inc.
P.O. Box 1280
Albuquerque, New Mexico 87103

**Pennsylvania**   Ms. Linda Meyer, Acting Director
Center for Rape Concern
Philadelphia General Hospital
34th Street and Civic Center Blvd.
Philadelphia, Pennsylvania 19104

**Tennessee**   Gene G. Abel, M.D., Director
Program for Sexual Offenders
Department of Psychiatry
College of Medicine
University of Tennessee
P.O. Box 4966
Memphis, Tennessee 38104

**Washington**   N. Nichols, Director
Treatment Program for the Sexual Offender
Western State Hospital
Fort Steilacoom, Washington 98494

Robert W. Deisher, M.D.
Juvenile Sex Offender Program
Adolescent Clinic
Division of Adolescent Medicine
Room CD 287
CDMRC
University of Washington Hospital
Seattle, Washington 98105

# Notes

Chapter One

1. W. L. Cohen and R. J. Boucher, "Misunderstanding About Sex Criminals," *Sexual Behavior* 2, No. 2 (1972), p. 57.

2. Richard von Krafft-Ebing, *Psychopathia Sexualis* (Chicago: Login Brothers, 1922).

3. Menachem Amir, *Patterns in Forcible Rape* (Chicago: University of Chicago Press, 1971), p. 51.

4. Ibid., p. 72.

5. Ibid., pp. 339–340.

6. A. Teicher, L. DeFreitas, and A. Oshershon, "Group Psychology and the Intense Group Experience," *International Journal of Applied Behavior Science* 24, (April 1974), p. 162.

7. For further information write Dr. Robert Deisher, Juvenile Sex Offender Program Adolescent Clinic, CDMRC Clinical Training Unit, Room CD 287, University of Washington Hospital, Seattle, Washington 98105.

8. For further information write Dr. Nelson Handler, 819 Park Avenue, Baltimore, Maryland 21201.

9. P. H. Gebhard, J. H. Gangnon, W. B. Pomeroy, and C. V. Christenson, *Sex Offenders: An Analysis of Types* (New York: Harper & Row, 1965).

10. Frances Wilckes, *The Inner World of Children* (New York: New American Library, 1966), p. 128.


## Chapter Two

1. Menachem Amir, *Patterns in Forcible Rape* (Chicago: University of Chicago Press, 1971).

2. Frances Wilckes, *The Inner World of Children* (New York: New American Library, 1966).

3. Amir, op. cit.


## Chapter Three

1. Pamphlet, "National Center for the Prevention and Control of Rape," National Institute of Mental Health, Rockville, Maryland.

2. Edward Brecher, "Treatment Programs for Sex Offenders" (January 1977), National Institute of Law Enforcement and Criminal Justice, U.S. Department of Justice, Washington, D.C.

3. Synanon was the first self-help drug addiction program.


## Chapter Four

1. Richard Seely, The Treatment Program for Sexual Offenders, Western State Hospital, Fort Steilacoom, Washington (St. Peter, Minnesota: 1974).

2. G. J. McDonald and G. de Furia, "A Guided Self-Help Approach to the Habitual Sex Offender," *Hospital and Community Psychiatry* (October 1971), pp. 22 and 311, cited in Larry Hendricks, *Some Effective Change-Inducing Mechanisms in Operation in the Specialized Treatment Program for Sex Offenders* (State of Washington, Department of Social and Health Services, April 1975).

3. Seely, op. cit.

4. Richard Seely, *Brief Description of Intensive Treatment Program for Sexual Aggressives, Minnesota Security Hospital* (St. Peter, Minnesota: 1977).

5. Edward Brecher, "Treatment Programs for Sex Offenders" (Washington, D.C.: National Institute of Law Enforcement and Criminal Justice, U.S. Department of Justice, January 1977).

Chapter Five

1. William Glasser, *Reality Therapy* (New York: Harper & Row, 1965).

2. Edward Brecher, "Treatment Program for Sex Offenders" (Washington, D.C.: National Institute of Law Enforcement and Criminal Justice, January 1977).

3. William Hausman, "Report on Sex Offenders: A Sociological, Psychiatric, and Psychological Study," Minneapolis: University of Minnesota (December 1972).


Chapter Six

1. Jerrold K. Footlick, "Rape Alert," *Newsweek*, November 10, 1975, pp. 77–78.


Chapter Seven

1. Jerrold K. Footlick, "Rape Alert," *Newsweek*, November 10, 1975, pp. 77–78.

2. "To Establish Justice, to Insure Domestic Tranquility," final report of the National Commission on the Causes and Prevention of Violence, 1969, pp. 19, 28. This report was directed to the President of the United States. It is a government document for sale by the Superintendent of Documents: PR 36.8:V81 J98-2.


Chapter Eight

1. Germaine Greer, "Seduction Is a Four-Letter Word," *Playboy* (January 1973), p. 2.


Chapter Nine

1. *The New England Journal of Medicine*, October 6, 1977, pp. 764–767.

2. Marvin Frankel, *Criminal Sentences* (New York: Hill and Wang, 1972), pp. 15 and 16.

3. Ibid., p. 21.

4. Norval Morris, *The Honest Politician's Guide to Crime Control* (Chicago: University of Chicago Press, 1970), as cited by Melvin

Goldberg during the symposia "The Sex Offender: Are We All Victims?" held in twelve Minnesota cities, 1976–1977.

5. Harry Elmer Barnes, *The Story of Punishment* (Boston: Stratford Company, 1930), p. 265, as cited in Frankel, op. cit., pp. 53–54.


## Chapter Ten

1. Marvin Frankel, *Criminal Sentences* (New York: Hill and Wang, 1972), p. ix.

2. Ibid., p. iii.

3. Melvin Goldberg is a law professor at the William Mitchell Law School in St. Paul, Minnesota. He was the keynote speaker at the symposia "The Sex Offender: Are We All Victims?"

4. Memphis, Tennessee, April 14, 1977, First Annual Conference on the Treatment of Sexual Aggressives.

5. William Glasser, *Reality Therapy* (New York: Harper & Row, 1965), p. 93.

6. Dale E. Swenson, "Violence!" *American Journal of Corrections* (January-February 1975), p. 35.


## Appendix B

1. B. L. Glueck, Jr., "Final Report: Research for the Study of Persons Convicted of Crimes Involving Sexual Aberrations" (June 1955, June 1956).

2. Dr. Richard Chilgren describes this program in chapter four.

3. W. L. Cohen and R. J. Boucher, "Misunderstanding About Sex Criminals," *Sexual Behavior* 2, No. 2 (1972), pp. 56–62.

# Bibliography

Amir, Menachem. *Patterns in Forcible Rape*. Chicago: University of Chicago Press, 1971.

Brecher, Edward. "Treatment Programs for Sex Offenders." National Institute of Law Enforcement and Criminal Justice, U.S. Department of Justice, Washington, D.C., January 1977.

Brownmiller, Susan. *Against Our Will*. New York: Simon and Schuster, 1975.

Cohen, Murray; Seghorn, Theofaris; and Calmas, Wilfred. "Sociometric Study of The Sex Offenders." *Journal of Abnormal Psychology*, 1969.

Ellis, Havelock. *Studies in Psychology of Sex*. Vols. I, II. New York: Random House, 1905.

Erikson, Erik. *Childhood and Society*. 2nd rev. ed. Boston: W. W. Norton, 1963.

Footlick, Jerrold K. "Rape Alert!" *Newsweek*, November 10, 1975.

Frankel, Marvin E. *Criminal Sentencing*. New York: Hill and Wang, 1972.

Glasser, William. *Reality Therapy*. New York: Harper & Row, 1965.

Green, Robert L. *The Urban Challenge—Poverty and Race*. Chicago: Follet Publishing Company, 1977.

Greer, Germaine. "Seduction is a Four-Letter Word." *Playboy*, January 1973.

Harris, Marvin. "Why Men Dominate Women." *New York Times Magazine,* November 13, 1977.

Hausman, William. "Report on Sex Offenders: A Sociological, Psychiatric, and Psychological Study." Minneapolis: University of Minnesota, December 1972.

Hendricks. Larry. *Some Effective Change-Inducing Mechanisms in Operation in the Specialized Treatment Program for Sex Offenders.* State of Washington Department of Social and Health Services, April 1975.

Janov, Arthur. *Primal Scream.* New York: Putnam, 1970.

Krafft-Ebing, Dr. Richard von. *Psychopathia Sexualis.* Rev. ed. Chicago: Login Brothers, 1931.

Lieberman, M. A. "Up the Right Mountain, Down the Wrong Path." *Journal of Applied Behavioral Science* 10, No. 2, April 1974, pp. 156–174.

Macindoe, Dr. Ian. "Some Thoughts About the Criminal Process." Unpublished paper, St. Peter, Minnesota, 1975.

Macindoe, Ian, and Pengelly, Earlyn. *The Behavioral, Emotional, and Attitudinal Development Program for Sex Offenders at the Minnesota Security Hospital, 1974–75.* Booklet. St. Peter, Minnesota, 1975. For reprints contact Ms. Earlyn Pengelly, Minnesota Security Hospital, 2000 South Minnesota Ave., St. Peter, Minn. 56082.

Meehl, Dr. Paul. "Sex Offenders and the Criminal Process." Unpublished paper, 1975.

Mitford, Jessica. *Kind and Usual Punishment.* New York: Knopf, 1973.

National Center for the Prevention and Control of Rape, *Rape Prevention—A New National Center.* Pamphlet printed by the organization, 5600 Fishers Lane, Rockville, Md. 20852.

Parker, Tony. *The Twisting Lane: The Hidden World of Sex Offenders.* New York: Harper & Row, 1969.

Rachin, Richard L. "Reality Therapy: Helping People Help Themselves," January-February 1975.

Seely, Richard. "The Treatment Program for Sexual Offenders. Western State Hospital, Fort Steilacoom, Washington." Unpublished paper, St. Peter, Minnesota, 1974.

"Intensive Program for Sexual Aggressives," Unpublished paper, St. Peter, Minnesota, 1977.

Swenson, Dale E. "Violence!" *American Journal of Corrections*, January-February 1975.

Wasserman, Michelle. "Rape: Breaking the Silence." *The Progressive*, November 1973.

Wilckes, Frances G. *The Inner World of Childhood*. New York: New American Library, 1966.

Wilson, James Q. "Changing Criminal Sentences." *Harper's Magazine*, November 1977.

Wilson, Lance. "Sex Offenders and Their Treatment in Minnesota (Minneapolis, Minn., 1978).

*Understanding the Psychopathic Personality*. Western State Hospital at Fort Steilacoom, Washington. A pamphlet distributed and written by the Hospital, 1975.

# Index